JAP
YOU

A Headway phrasebook

Colin Lloyd and Etsuko Tsujita

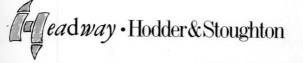

Headway · Hodder & Stoughton

British Library Cataloguing in Publication Data

Lloyd, Colin
  Japanese in your pocket: book. – (In your pocket)
  I. Title   II. Tsujita, Etsuko   III. Series
  495.6

ISBN 0 0340 54216 0

First published 1992

Typeset by Master Typesetters
Printed in Hong Kong for the educational publishing
division of Hodder & Stoughton Ltd, Mill Road,
Dunton Green, Sevenoaks, Kent by Colorcraft Ltd.

Contents

Introduction   4
Pronunciation Guide   5
Basic Grammar   10
Basic Expressions   13
Arrival and Departure   17
Accommodation   25
Eating Out   33
Entertainment and Sport   49
Health   65
Travel   73
Shopping   97
Services   113
Essential Information   129
Wordlist   144

Introduction

There is no doubt that there has recently been a
dramatic increase in interest in all things Japanese. The
people, culture, business methods and modernistic
outlook have had a great deal of exposure in the
media. More people than ever are coming into contact
with Japan and feel that a basic knowledge of the
language and some insight into the culture would be a
useful asset. *Japanese in your pocket* has been written
to meet precisely those needs. Whether you are a
tourist in this fascinating country or doing business
with the Japanese, you will find *Japanese in your
pocket* indispensable as a means of getting by in the
language.

This book is conveniently divided into easily
referenced sections which supply appropriate phrases
along with useful information. For those with no prior
knowledge of Japanese, a basic grammar section can
be found on page 10, and the pronunciation guide on
page 5 will also give the beginner an introduction to
the sounds of Japanese. Japanese script is given
throughout, so if you have difficulties making yourself
understood, you can point to the phrase in the book.

The Japanese are always delighted to meet foreigners,
and are very impressed with anyone who makes an
effort to speak what they, with good reason, think is a
very unique language. The message has to be:
persevere and . . .

GANBATTE

Pronunciation Guide

- This book gives phrases both in Japanese script and the anglicised form of Japanese known as *romaji*. This approximates Japanese sounds to those we are familiar with in English, but remember that this can never be completely accurate, and you should listen to native speakers or the cassette that accompanies this book to improve your pronunciation. It would be a good idea to familiarise yourself with the following pages before tackling the phrases.

Vowel sounds

- There are five vowel sounds:

a	as in **a**pple
i	as in p**i**ano
u	as in tr**u**e
e	as in r**e**d
o	as in g**o**

- These are usually short and sharp sounds, but if the vowel carries a bar eg, ō, the vowel is elongated, ie it doubles in length but without any change in the sound.

Consonants

- The consonants are pronounced much as they are in English with the following exceptions:

g	is always hard as in **good** and never soft as in **gender**.
l	doesn't exist as a sound in Japanese and is always pronounced as an **r**, so London is pronounced 'rondon'.
n	when it comes at the end of a word has a very nasal sound, and is not rounded off by touching the back of the front teeth with the tongue.
f	is much softer in Japanese – more of a breath than an 'f'. When making the sound in Japanese, the front teeth don't touch the lower lip. e.g. Mount Fuji becomes *Huji – yama*.

- It's worth noting that the words *desu* and *masu* which you will come across very frequently in Japanese, are pronounced *dess* and *mass* respectively.
- Stress is not particularly important in the Japanese sentence. All syllables are given roughly equal weighting, but people tend to speak very fast, so it is worth learning the phrase 'Speak slowly please' (see page 14).

The Japanese Syllabary and Kanji

- The syllabary is a group of symbols where each symbol represents a syllable.
- Written Japanese is a compound of the syllabary containing *Katakana*, *Hiragana* and *Kanji*. *Kanji* are the ideograms taken from Chinese with each character representing a word or an idea. There are some two to three thousand Kanji in everyday use and many thousands more waiting on the sidelines should they be required.
- The Katakana syllabary is used for writing words borrowed from foreign languages other than Chinese.

  e.g. タクシー ta-ku-shī = taxi
  　　　ビール 　bī-ru　　 = beer

  There are 46 basic syllables (see table on page 7) and numerous other syllables derived from them (see tables on pages 8 and 9).
- Hiragana is used to write verb and adjectival endings as well as particles. It is also used to facilitate reading amongst younger Japanese who have not acquired sufficient knowledge of Kanji. There are also 46 basic syllables in Hiragana along with their derivatives.
- A quick glance at ***Japanese in your pocket*** will show that a mixture of Katakana, Hiragana and Kanji are found in many Japanese sentences.

The Japanese Syllabary

ma ‗ ‗ ‗ ‗ ‗ ‗ ‗ Romaji
ま ‗ ‗ ‗ ‗ ‗ ‗ Hiragana
マ ‗ ‗ ‗ ‗ ‗ ‗ Katakana

a あ ア	i い イ	u う ウ	e え エ	o お オ
ka か カ	ki き キ	ku く ク	ke け ケ	ko こ コ
sa さ サ	shi し シ	su す ス	se せ セ	so そ ソ
ta た タ	chi ち チ	tsu つ ツ	te て テ	to と ト
na な ナ	ni に ニ	nu ぬ ヌ	ne ね ネ	no の ノ
ha は ハ	hi ひ ヒ	fu ふ フ	he へ へ	ho ほ ホ
ma ま マ	mi み ミ	mu む ム	me め メ	mo も モ
ya や ヤ		yu ゆ ユ		yo よ ヨ
ra ら ラ	ri り リ	ru る ル	re れ レ	ro ろ ロ
wa わ ワ				o を ヲ
n ん ン				

kya きゃ キャ	kyu きゅ キュ	kyo きょ キョ
sha しゃ シャ	shu しゅ シュ	sho しょ ショ
cha ちゃ チャ	chu ちゅ チュ	cho ちょ チョ
nya にゃ ニャ	nyu にゅ ニュ	nyo にょ ニョ
hya ひゃ ヒャ	hyu ひゅ ヒュ	hyo ひょ ヒョ
mya みゃ ミャ	myu みゅ ミュ	myo みょ ミョ
rya りゃ リャ	ryu りゅ リュ	ryo りょ リョ
gya ぎゃ ギャ	gyu ぎゅ ギュ	gyo ぎょ ギョ
ja じゃ ジャ	ju じゅ ジュ	jo じょ ジョ
bya びゃ ビャ	byu びゅ ビュ	byo びょ ビョ
pya ぴゃ ピャ	pyu ぴゅ ピュ	pyo ぴょ ピョ

ga が ガ	gi ぎ ギ	gu ぐ グ	ge げ ゲ	go ご ゴ
za ざ ザ	zi じ ジ	zu ず ズ	ze ぜ ゼ	zo ぞ ゾ
da だ ダ	ji ぢ ヂ	zu づ ヅ	de で デ	do ど ド

ba ば バ	bi び ビ	bu ぶ ブ	be べ ベ	bo ぼ ボ
pa ぱ パ	pi ぴ ピ	pu ぷ プ	pi ぺ ペ	po ぽ ポ

Basic Grammar

Word order

● The verb always comes at the end of the sentence:
Subject–object–verb
Kare wa tokei o motte imasu
He   wristwatch   has = He has a wristwatch

Verbs

● The most common verbs are:
desu which corresponds to the English verb 'to be',
so can mean 'am', 'are', 'is' etc.
Watashi wa Igirisu-jin desu
I   English   am = I am English
suru which means 'to do', is irregular. It is often
attached to nouns to make them into verbs:
benkyō suru = to do study = to study
ryokō suru = to do a journey = to travel
dansu suru = to do a dance = to dance

● Verbs often occur alone, without subject or object:
denwa shimasu = I am going to telephone someone

● *imasu* and *arimasu* are verbs which have no
equivalent in English, but can be roughly translated
as 'there is' or 'there are'. *imasu* denotes the
existence of animate objects and *arimasu* of
inanimate objects.
neko ga imasu   = There's a cat/There are some
cats

tsukue no ue ni
hon   = There is a book/There are
ga arimasu   books on the desk

● Verbs do not change their form according to the
same grammatical rules as English verbs.
Information about a verb is given by the particles
(see page 11).

Adjectives

● Japanese adjectives differ from English ones in that
they can sometimes function as verbs:
kono kēki wa **oishii** ne = This cake is **delicious**,
                                   isn't it?

- Two adjectives can be joined together using *kute*.

  O-sumō-san wa **ōkikute** *tsuyoi desu* = Sumo wrestlers are **big and strong**

  Shinkansen wa **hayakute benri** *desu* = The bullet train is **fast and convenient**

Adverbs

- Japanese adverbs work like English adverbs, modifying verbs and adjectives. The adjectival ending i changes to **ku**.

Particles

These are very important in Japanese, as they define the word which goes before them. Here are the most commonly used particles:

wa indicates that the noun or pronoun preceding it is the subject of the sentence.
Watashi **wa** *sensei desu* = I am a teacher

o indicates that the noun preceding it is the object of the verb that follows it.
Watashi wa **sake o** *nomimasu* = I drink *sake*

ga is a complex particle. One of its main functions is to replace *wa* when some emphasis is required.
Watashi **ga** *ikimasu* = I will go (implying 'I will go, you will stay')

no indicates possession after a preceding pronoun or noun
Kare no *kasa desu* = It's *his* umbrella
Kare-tachi no *kisha wa mō itte shimaimashita* = *Their* train has already gone

to corresponds to 'with' in English.
Watashi wa Howaito-san **to** *'sutēshon' to iu pabu e ikimashita*
I went to a pub called The Station **with** Mr White

e indicates direction and corresponds with 'to' in English.

Nagu-san no apāto e ikimashō ka
Shall we go **to** Mr Knagg's apartment?

ni   corresponds to the English prepositions 'on', 'in' and 'at'.
*Ichigatsu **ni*** = **in** January
*jū-ji **ni*** = **at** 10 c'clock
*Getsuyōbi **ni*** = **on** Monday

kara   corresponds to 'from' in English. *Kara . . . made* means 'from . . . to'
*Watashi no uchi **kara** sakaya **made** chodo ni hyaku-jū-mētoru desu*
From our house **to** the sake shop is exactly 210 metres

de   corresponds to 'at' or 'with'.
kamera de = **with** a camera
*Watashi wa **jinja de** Kenī-san ni aimashita* = I met Mr Kenny **at a shrine**

ka   at the end of a sentence indicates a question. For this reason there are no question marks in Japanese.

Basic expressions

yes	はい *hai*
no	いいえ *iie*
please	どうぞ *dōzo*
thank you (very much)	ありがとう（ございます） *arigatō (gozaimasu)*
Don't mention it	どういたしまして *dō itashimashite*
I'm sorry	すみません／御免なさい *sumimasen/gomen-nasai*
Excuse me	すみません／失礼ですが *sumimasen/shitsurei desu ga*
hello	こんにちは *konnichiwa*
goodbye	さようなら *sayōnara*
Good morning	おはよう（ございます） *ohayō (gozaimasu)*
Good afternoon	こんにちは *konnichiwa*
Good evening	こんばんは *konbanwa*
Good night	おやすみ（なさい） *o-yasumi (nasai)*
How are you?	お元気ですか／ごきげんいかがですか *o-genki desu ka/go-kigen ikaga desu Ka*
How do you do?	はじめまして／ごきげんいかがですか *hajimemashite/go-kigen ikaga desu ka*
This is Mr/Mrs/Miss...	こちらは...さんです *kochira wa...san desu*

13

Basic Expressions

Help!	助けて *tasukete*
I feel ill	気分が悪いです *kibun ga warui desu*
How much is it?	いくらですか *ikura desu ka*
What does that mean?	それはどういう意味ですか *sore wa dō iu imi desu ka*
I don't know	わかりません *wakarimasen*
I don't speak Japanese	私は日本語を話しません *Watashi wa nihon—go o hanashimasen*
Could you speak more slowly?	もっとゆっくり話していただけますか *motto yukkuri hanashite itadakemasu ka*
Please say it again	もう一度お願いします *mō ichi-do o-negai shimasu*
I don't understand	わかりません *wakarimasen*
Do you speak English?	英語を話しますか *eigo o hanashimasu ka*
Where are (the toilets)?	便所／トイレ／手洗いはどこですか *(benjo／toire／tearai) wa doko desu ka*
What is it?	それは何ですか *sore wa nan desu ka*
It's . . .	(それは) . . . です *(sore wa) . . . desu*
who?	誰／どなた *dare／donata*
when?	いつ *itsu*

Basic Expressions

where?	どこ *doko*
what?	何 *nani*
how?	どのように *dono yō ni*
which?	どれ／どちら *dore/dochira*
why?	なぜ／どうして *naze/dōshite*
What's the time?	今、何時ですか *ima, nan-ji desu ka*
How old are you?	何才ですか *nan-sai desu ka*
I/we	私／私達 *watashi/watashi-tachi*
you/you (plural)	あなた／あなた達 *anata/anata-tachi*
he/they	彼／彼等 *kare/kare-ra*
she/they	彼女／彼女等 *kanojo/kanojo-ra*
this/these	これ／これら *kore/kore-ra*
it, that /those	それ／それら *sore/sore-ra*
that (over there)/those (over there)	あれ／あれら *are/are-ra*
here/there/over there	ここ／そこ／あそこ *koko/soko/asoko*
I like...	が好きです *...ga suki desu*
I hate...	が嫌いです *...ga kirai desu*

15

Basic Expressions

good/bad	良い／悪い *yoi/warui*
I'd like...	お願いします *...o-negai shimasu*
I want...	が欲しいです *...ga hoshii desu*
more/less	より多い／より少ない *yori ōi/yori sukunai*
better/worse	より良い／より悪い *yori yoi/yori warui*
too much/too little	多すぎる／少なすぎる *ō-sugiru/sukuna-sugiru*
Can I...?	できますか *...dekimasu ka*
Must I...?	しなければなりませんか *...shinakereba narimasen ka*
Will you...?	して下さいますか *...shite kudasaimasu ka*
May I...?	しても良いですか *...shite mo ii desu ka*
Let's...	さあ...しましょう *sa...shimashō*
Please give me...	を下さい *...o kudasai*

- The Japanese use the word *-san* after the family name, eg, *Tanaka-san, Tsujita-san. San* can mean Mr, Mrs, Miss or Ms.
- The Japanese very often omit pronouns altogether. *Tanaka desu* means 'I am (Mr or Mrs) Tanaka'.
- Never use *san* after your own name. Don't say *Watashi wa Jōnzu-san desu*, only *Watashi wa Jōnzu desu*.
- You are always on safe ground using *san*. You will also hear *chan* when adults are referring to their own children or other people's children with whom they are familiar.

ARRIVAL
AND
DEPARTURE

- You will almost certainly arrive in Japan at either Tokyo (東京) or Osaka (大阪) International Airports. Everything is signposted in English, eg Customs (税関) and Immigration (出入国管理). There are quite often lengthy delays at Immigration.
- It is advisable to use the airport – city-centre buses in either city. Narita airport in particular is a long distance from Tokyo and could prove to be very expensive by taxi.
- You will find medium-priced hotels close to the airport if you need them.
- If you take a taxi, there is no need to tip the driver, and the cost of the toll for the expressway is automatically added to your fare. Taxi drivers are almost always scrupulously honest, and will not try to cheat you.
- 'Loop lines' are an indispensable form of urban

transport. They are like ring roads in the local rail system, circling the city centre. In Tokyo the loop line is called *Yamanote-sen* and in Osaka it's *Kanjo-sen*.

Asking the way

Excuse me, where is/are...?	すみません、...はどこですか *sumimasen, ...wa doko desu ka*
...the bar	バー／酒場 *...bā/sakaba...*
...the bus stop	バスの停留所（バス停） *...basu no teiryū-jo (basu-tei)...*
...the car park	駐車場 *...chūsha-jō...*
...the coffee shop	喫茶店 *...kissa-ten...*
...the entrance/exit	入口／出口 *...iriguchi/deguchi...*
...the emergency exit	非常口 *...hijō-guchi...*
...the exchange bureau	両替所 *...ryōgae-jo...*
...the information desk	案内所／受付 *...annai-jo/uketsuke...*
...the left luggage office	手荷物一時預り所 *...te-nimotsu ichiji azukari-jo...*
...the loop line	環状線 *...kanjō-sen...*
...the restaurant	レストラン／食堂 *...resutoran/shokudō...*

. . . the taxi stand	タクシーのりば
	. . . *takushī noriba* . . .
. . . ticket machines	切符販売機
	. . . *kippu hanbai-ki* . . .
. . . the ticket office	切符売場
	. . . *kippu uriba* . . .
. . . toilets	トイレ／お便所／お手洗い
	. . . *toire/o-benjo/o-tearai*
. . . the underground	地下鉄
	. . . *chika-tetsu* . . .
. . . the waiting room	待合室
	. . . *machiai-shitsu* . . .

Where's the nearest (station/post office)?
最寄りの(駅／郵便局)はどこですか

moyori no (eki/yūbin-kyoku) wa doko desu ka

Is there a bus stop near here?
この近くにバス停がありますか

kono chikaku ni basu-tei ga arimasu ka

Where can I hire a car?
どこでレンタカーが借りられますか

doko de renta-kā ga kariraremasu ka

Where should I go to find lost property?
落し物を捜すにはどこにいけばいいですか

otoshimono o sagasu niwa doko ni ikeba ii desu ka

How do I get to. . .?
へは、どう行けばいいですか

. . . ewa, dō ikeba ii desu ka

How far away is the. . .?
までどの位の距離がありますか

. . . made dono kurai no kyori ga arimasu ka

Is it far?
遠いですか
tōi desu ka

19

Could you repeat that, please?	それを繰り返していただけますか *sore o kurikaeshite itadakemasu ka*
Could you speak more slowly?	もっとゆっくり話していただけますか *motto yukkuri hanashite itadakemasu ka*
I didn't understand	わかりませんでした *wakarimasen deshita*

You may hear:

を行って下さい *...o itte kudasai*	Take...
最初の道 *...saisho no michi*	...the first street
二番目の道 *...ni-banme no michi*	...the second street
右側／右手 *...migi-gawa/migi-te*	...on the right
左側／左手 *...hidari-gawa/hidari-te*	...on the left
まっすぐ行って下さい *massugu itte kudasai*	Go straight on
右に曲って下さい *migi ni magatte kudasai*	Turn right
左に曲って下さい *hidari ni magatte kudasai*	Turn left
この道の終点に（で） *kono michi no shūten ni (de)*	at the end of the street
2km 程離れた所にあります *ni-kiromētoru hodo hanareta tokoro ni arimasu*	It's about two kilometres away

Luggage

Where are the trolleys?	手押し車はどこにありますか *teoshi-guruma wa doko ni arimasu ka*
I can't find...	が見つかりません *...ga mitsukarimasen.*
...my handbag	私のハンドバッグ *...watashi no hando-baggu*
...my luggage	私の荷物 *...watashi no nimotsu*
...my suitcase (s)	私のスーツケース *...watashi no sūtsu-kēsu*
Could you take it/them to...?	それを...まで運んでいただけますか *sore o...made hakonde itadakemasu ka*
...the exit	出口 *...deguchi...*
...the luggage lockers	コインロッカー *...koin rokkā...*
...platform number 2	2番線ホーム *...ni-bansen hōmu...*
...the taxi stand	タクシーのりば *...takushī noriba...*

At the information desk

Could you give me...?	をいただけますか *...o itadakemasu ka*
...a brochure on this town	この町のパンフレット *...kono machi no panfuretto*

. . . a map of the city	この市の地図 . . . *kono shi no chizu*
. . . a list of hotels	ホテルの一覧表 . . . *hoteru no ichiran-hyō*

Getting a taxi

Where can I get a taxi?	どこでタクシーが拾えますか *doko de takushī ga hiroemasu ka*
Where is the taxi stand?	タクシーのりばはどこですか *takushī noriba wa doko desu ka*

I want to go to. . .	へ行きたいのですが、 . . . *e ikitai no desu ga*

. . . this address	この住所 *kono jūsho. . .*
. . . the airport	空港 *kūkō. . .*
. . . the bus station	バス停留所 *basu teiryū-jo. . .*
. . . the railway station	鉄道駅 *tetsudō-eki. . .*
. . . the hotel	ホテル *hoteru. . .*

Can you go more slowly?	もっとゆっくり行って下さい *motto yukkuri itte kudasai*
Stop here, please	ここで止まって下さい *koko de tomatte kudasai*
Will you wait here, please?	ここで待っていて下さい *koko de matte ite kudasai*
How much is it?	いくらですか *ikura desu ka*

Can you go a little faster?

もう少し急いで下さい
mō sukoshi isoide kudasai

I want to catch the 3 o'clock train

3時の汽車に乗りたいのですが

san-ji no kisha ni noritai no desu ga

Could you help me with my luggage?

荷物を運んで下さい
nimotsu o hakonde kudasai

At customs

I'm British

私は英国人です
watashi wa eikoku-jin desu

I'm American

私はアメリカ人です
watashi wa amerika-jin desu

I'm here . . .

来ました
. . . kimashita

. . . on business

仕事で
shigoto de . . .

. . . on holiday

休暇で
kyūka de . . .

. . . to visit my friends

友達に会いに
tomodachi ni ai ni . . .

I'm staying here (for one week/for a month)

（一週間／一ヶ月）滞在の予定です

(is-shūkan/ik-kagetsu) taizai no yotei desu

I'll be staying at this address

この住所に滞在します
kono jūsho ni taizai shimasu

I've lost my passport

パスポートを失しました
pasupōto o nakushimashita

I have nothing to declare

申告するものは何もありません

shinkoku suru mono wa nani mo arimasen

I've got . . .	を持っています . . . o motte imasu
. . . a bottle of whisky	ウイスキー一本 uisukī ip-pon . . .
. . . cigarettes / perfume	煙草／香水 . . . tabako/kōsui
It's for my personal use	（それは）私用に使います (sore wa) shiyō ni tsukaimasu

You may hear:

パスポートを見せて下さい pasupōto o misete kudasai	May I see your passport?
あなたの姓名は（何ですか） anata no seimei wa (nan desu ka)	What's your name?
あなたの国籍は（何ですか） anata no kokuseki wa (nan desu ka)	What nationality are you?
どの位滞在の予定ですか dono kurai taizai no yotei desu ka	How long are you going to stay?
荷物を見せて下さい nimotsu o misete kudasai	Show me your luggage, please
日本で何を購入しましたか nihon de nani o kōnyu shimashita ka	What have you bought in Japan?
どこで／いつ　それを買いましたか doko de/itsu sore o kaimashita ka	Where/When did you buy it?
（それは）いくらでしたか (sore wa) ikura deshita ka	How much did it cost?
何も申告する物はありませんか nani mo shinkoku suru mono wa arimasen ka	Have you anything to declare?

ACCOMMODATION

There are various types of accommodation available for the visitor to Japan:

- *Minshuku* （民宿） Traditional, small, family-run guest houses. These are fairly basic, but offer reasonably priced accommodation.
- *Ryokan* （旅館） Traditional Japanese hotels. They are more expensive than *Minshukus*, and generally they justify their higher prices. They usually have large bathrooms and supply *yukata* (cotton robes) as a matter of course.
- Western Style Hotels （ホテル） As you would expect, standards and prices vary enormously, but you should expect and get value for money in terms of service and courtesy.
- Business Hotels （ビジネスホテル） The less expensive type of western hotel. They are useful for emergencies or if you are short of money.

- Youth Hostels (ユースホステル)   Good value, but thin on the ground compared with western Youth Hostels. You should book well in advance in the summer.
- Love Hotels (ラブホテル)   Simply for couples who need privacy.

Business hotels are quite a new idea. Essentially they cater for the Japanese businessmen (they invariably refer to themselves as *Sararīmen*–Salarymen) who want a clean, convenient, moderately priced place to stay overnight.

The rooms are usually furnished with a bed (instead of a futon), a telephone, a desk and perhaps a refrigerator (*reizoko*) stocked with all kinds of drinks. Should the foreign business visitor decide to stay in a business hotel, they have to remember that neither English nor any other foreign language is likely to be spoken. According to the Japan National Tourist Organisation, these hotels are only located in the city centres, and not in other resorts. There's no room service, but there's usually a small restaurant available.

Registration

- You might be asked to fill in a registration form and hand over your passport, which will be returned to you after the details have been taken.

You may see:

御氏名／御住所 *go-shimei/go-jūsho*	name/address
ご連絡先 *go-renraku-saki*	contact address
生年月日／生誕地 *seinen gappi/seitan-chi*	date/place of birth
旅券番号 *ryoken bangō*	passport number
署名／日付 *shomei/hizuke*	signature/date

Accommodation

Is there a hotel near here?	この辺にホテルはありますか *kono hen ni hoteru wa arimasu ka*
My name is...	(私の名前は)...です *(Watashi no namae wa)...desu*
I have a reservation	予約はしてあります *yoyaku wa shite arimasu*
Is it expensive?	高いですか *takai desu ka*
We're staying for one night	一泊したいんですが *ip-paku shitai n desu ga*
There are two of us	私達二人です *watashi-tachi futari desu*

At a hotel

Have you any rooms?	空室は　ありますか *kūshitsu wa arimasu ka*
No, I haven't booked	いいえ　予約は、していません *iie, yoyaku wa shite imasen*
I'd like to book a room	・部屋の予約をしたいのですが *heya no yoyaku o shitai no desu ga*
What is the cost of a room...?	部屋は、いくらですか *...heya wa ikura desu ka*
...for one/two	一人／二人　用の *hitori/futari yō no...*
...for a family	家族用の *kazoku yō no...*
...with one/two bed	ベットが　1つ／2つ　ある *betto ga hitotsu/futatsu aru...*
...with a double bed	ダブルベットが一つある *daburu betto ga hitotsu, aru...*

Accommodation

. . . with an extra bed	余分にベットがある *yobun ni betto ga aru . . .*
. . . with/without a shower	シャワーが ある／ない *shawā ga aru/nai . . .*
. . . with/without a bathroom	浴室が ある／ない *yokushitsu ga aru/nai . . .*
. . . with a toilet	トイレ／WCがある *toire/WC ga aru . . .*

Our party consists of two adults and three children	私達一行は大人二人子供三人です *Watashi-tachi ikkō wa otona futari kodomo san-nin desu*

How much is it . . . ?	いくらですか *. . . ikura desu ka*

. . . per day	一日に付き *ichi-nichi ni tsuki . . .*
. . . per person	一人に付き *hitori ni tsuki . . .*
. . . per night	一泊に付き *ip-paku ni tsuki . . .*
. . . weekly	一週間に付き *is-shūkan ni tsuki . . .*
. . . for half-board	一泊朝食付き *ip-paku chōshoku tsuki . . .*
. . . for full-board	一泊二食付き *ip-paku ni-shoku tsuki . . .*

Is breakfast included?	朝食は入っていますか *choshōku wa haitte imasu ka*
Are tax and service included?	税金とサービス料は入っていますか *zeikin to sābisu-ryō wa haitte imasu ka*

Accommodation

Is there a reduced rate for children?	子供用の割引はありますか *kodomo yō no waribiki wa arimasu ka*
Is there a lift (elevator)?	エレベーターはありますか *erebēta wa arimasu ka*
It's too expensive	（値段が）高過ぎます *(nedan ga) taka-sugimasu*
Have you anything cheaper?	もっと安いのがありますか *motto yasui no ga arimasu ka*
We'll take them, please	私達にそれを下さい。 *watashi-tachi ni sore o kudasai*
We're leaving on Sunday	私達は日曜日に出発します *watashi-tachi wa nichiyōbi ni shuppatsu shimasu*

At what time do you serve...?	何時に...を食べますか *nan-ji ni...o tabemasu ka*
..breakfast	朝食 *...chōshoku...*
..lunch	昼食 *...chūshoku...*
..dinner	夕食 *...yūshoku...*

How far away is...?	までどの位ありますか *...made dono kurai arimasu ka*
..the beach	海岸 *kaigan...*
..the railway station	鉄道駅 *tetsudō-eki...*
..the town centre	市，町の中心街 *shi, machi no chūshingai...*

May I have...?	（を）いただけないでしょうか ...o itadakenai deshō ka
...the bill (the check)	勘定書 kanjō-sho...
...a key	鍵 kagi...
...an extra pillow	枕もう一つ makura mō hitotsu...
...some soap	石鹼 sekken...
...a towel	手ぬぐい／タオル tenugui/taoru...
...an ashtray	灰皿 haizara...
...an extra blanket	毛布もう一枚 mōfu mō ichi-mai...
...some writing paper	筆記用紙 hikki yōshi...
...some toilet paper	トイレットペーパー toiretto pēpā...

You may hear:

予約をなさいましたか **yoyaku o nasaimashita ka**	Have you made a reservation?
何か身分の証明になるような物をお持ちですか **nanika mibun no shōmei ni naru yō na mono o o-mochi desu ka**	Have you any identification?
食事は入っていません **shokuji wa haitte imasen**	Meals are not included
エレベーターは、ありません **erebētā wa arimasen**	There isn't a lift (elevator)

Accommodation

この用紙に記入していただけますか *kono yōshi ni kinyū shite itadakemasu ka*	Would you fill in this form?
ここにサインしてください *koko ni sain shite kudasai*	Sign here, please
どの位ご滞在の予定ですか *dono kurai go-taizai no yotei desu ka*	How long are you staying?
空室はありません *kūshitsu wa arimasen*	There is no room

Room service

Could you bring breakfast to my room?	朝食を私の部屋に運んでいただけますか *chōshoku o watashi no heya ni hakonde itadakemasu ka*
Do you have foreign newspapers?	外国の新聞はありますか *gaikoku no shinbun wa arimasu ka*
Can you give me an early morning call?	朝早くモーニングコールをして頂けますか *asa hayaku mōningu kōru o shite itadakemasu ka*
Do you have a fax machine I could use?	私が使えるファクシミリの機械はありますか *watashi ga tsukaeru fakushimiri no kikai wa arimasu ka*
Could you send this fax for me?	このファクシミリを送って頂けますか *kono fakushimiri o okutte itadakemasu ka*
Is there a laundry service?	洗濯はして頂けますか *sentaku wa shite itadakemasu ka*

I'd like to call . . .	に電話を掛けたいんです が
	. . . ni denwa o kaketai n. desu ga
. . . New York	ニューヨーク
	Nyūyōku . . .
. . . London	ロンドン
	Rondon . . .

Checking out

May I have the bill please?	お勘定して下さい
	o-kanjō shite kudasai
Is everything included?	全部含まれていますか
	zenbu fukumarete imasu ka
Can I pay by credit card?	クレジットカードで払って いいですか
	kurejitto kādo de haratte mo ii desu ka
Can you call us a taxi?	タクシーを呼んで頂けますか
	takushī o yonde itadakemasu ka
Could we have our passports please?	パスポートを頂けますか
	pasupōto o itadakemasu ka
I must leave immediately	私はすぐ出発しなければなり ません
	watashi wa sugu shuppatsu shinakereba narimasen
I think there's a mistake on the bill	この勘定書は間違っていると 思いますが
	kono kanjō-sho wa machigatte iru to omoimasu ga
Can I have a receipt?	領収書を頂けますか
	ryōshū-sho o itadakemasu ka

EATING OUT

- There is a bewildering variety of restaurants to be found in Japanese cities. Many are found clustered around the railway and/or underground stations.
- Coffee shops often serve hot, simple meals (fried rice or noodle dishes) as well as sandwiches and other snacks.
- Station platforms often have restaurants that serve fast food for the traveller in a hurry, as do the street stands (屋台 *yatai*). Look out for very inexpensive food at the stand-up bars (立ち飲み屋 *tachinomi-ya*).
- The most expensive meals are served in beef restaurants and restaurants that don't display any prices. Many restaurants have plastic replicas of their dishes displayed in glass cases at the entrance with the price clearly written.

Eating Out

- Sushi shop prices vary – you usually get value for money. Prices are often higher nearer the city centre.
- All culinary tastes are catered for, although it may take a while to find the various European, Chinese, Korean and Indian restaurants. American 'drive-in' family restaurants seem to be on the increase.
- There are fixed-price dishes 定食 *teishoku* (usually with rice and miso soup), but more often than not you will be ordering à la carte almost wherever you are. Very popular types are *robatayaki* 炉端焼 (charcoal grill restaurants) *yakitoriya* 焼鳥屋 (chicken specialist restaurants) or *sushiya* 寿司屋 (sushi shops).
- There's no need to tip in a restaurant. To avoid embarrassment, avoid tipping altogether.

I'm hungry	お腹がすきました *onaka ga sukimashita*
I'm thirsty	喉が渇きました *nodo ga kawakimashita*
Is there a good restaurant near here?	この辺にいいレストランはありますか *kono hen ni ii resutoran wa arimasu ka*
Are there any inexpensive sushi shops?	値段が安いお寿司屋はありますか *nedan ga yasui o-sushi-ya wa arimasu ka*
I'd like to reserve a table for six	六人用のテーブルを予約したいのですが *roku-nin yo no teburu o yoyaku shitai no desu ga*
Can we come at 7.30?	七時半にお願いします *shichi-ji han ni o-negai shimasu*

Eating Out

Could we sit...?	私達は . . . にすわってもいい ですか *watashi-tachi wa . . . ni* *suwatte mo ii desu ka*
. . .at the counter	カウンターに . . .*kauntā ni*. . .
. . .in the corner	コーナー／隅 に . . .*kōnā/sumi ni*. . .
. . .in a non-smoking area	禁煙区域に . . .*kin'en kuiki ni*. . .
. . .by the window	窓の側に . . .*mado no soba ni*. . .

Ordering snacks

Please give me...	下さい . . .*kudasai*
I'd like...	お願いします . . .*o-negai shimasu*
. . .a beer	ビール1本 *bīru ip-pon*. . .
. . .two iced coffees	アイスコーヒー2つ *aisu kōhī futatsu*. . .
. . .a hot coffee	ホットコーヒー1つ *hotto (kōhī) hitotsu*. . .
. . .a fruit juice	フルーツジュース1つ *furūtsu jūsu hitotsu*. . .
. . .a hamburger	ハンバーガー1個 *hanbāgā ik-ko*. . .
. . .a toasted cheese and ham sandwich	チーズとハムのサンドトース ト *chīzu to hamu no sando* *tōsuto*. . .

...curry rice	カレーライス *karē raisu...*
...spaghetti	スパゲッティ *supagetti...*
...fried rice	焼き飯 *yaki-meshi...*
...fried noodles	焼きそば *yaki-soba...*
What sort of sandwiches do you have?	どんなサンドイッチがありますか *donna sandoitchi ga arimasu ka*
I'll have a ...sandwich	サンドを下さい *...sando o kudasai*
...egg/ham...	たまご／ハム *tamago/hamu...*
...mixed...	ミックス *mikkusu...*

Ordering a meal

Is there a table available, please?	テーブルはありますか *tēburu wa arimasu ka*
There are (two/three/four) of us	私達(二人／三人／四人)です *watashi-tachi (futari/san-nin/yo-nin) desu*
Will you bring me a menu?	メニューをお願いします *menyū o o-negai shimasu*
What shall we order?	何を頼みましょうか *nani o tanomimashō ka*
Excuse me (when calling the waiter/waitress)	すみません *sumimasen*
What do you recommend?	何がおいしいですか *nani ga oishii desu ka*

Eating Out

I'll have this	これを下さい *kore o kudasai*
Excuse me, I haven't got a . . .	すみません、... がありませんが *sumimasen, . . . ga arimasen ga*
. . . knife/fork/spoon	ナイフ／フォーク／スプーン *. . . naifu/fōku/supūn . . .*
. . . cup/glass/plate	カップ／グラス／お皿 *. . . kappu/gurasu/o-sara . . .*
That's enough	それで結構です *sore de kekkō desu*
Just a small portion	少しだけお願いします *sukoshi dake o-negai shimasu*

You may hear:

決まりましたか **kimarimashita ka**	Have you chosen?
他に何か **hoka ni nani ka**	Anything to follow?
お飲み物は何になさいますか **o-nomimono wa nani ni nasaimasu ka**	What would you like to drink?
ワインは赤と白とどちらがいいですか **wain wa aka to shiro to dochira ga ii desu ka**	Which wine do you prefer, red or white?
はありません **. . . wa arimasen**	We don't have any . . .
乾杯 **kanpai**	Cheers!

Describing food

It's tasty	おいしいです *oishii desu*
It's just right	ちょうどいいです *chōdo ii desu*
It's burnt	焦げています *kogete imasu*
It's overcooked	焼きすぎです／煮すぎです *yaki-sugi desu/ni-sugi desu*
It's well done	よく焼けています *yoku yakete imasu*
It's underdone	生焼けです *nama yake desu*
It's too salty	辛すぎます *kara-sugimasu*
It's too sweet	甘すぎます *ama-sugimasu*
This meat is (tough/tender)	この肉は（かたい／柔らかい）です *kono niku wa (katai/yawarakai) desu*
This is not fresh	これは新鮮ではありません *kore wa shinsen dewa arimasen*
It was very nice	とてもおいしかったです *totemo oishikatta desu*
I have enjoyed my dinner very much	ご馳走さまでした *go-chisō-sama deshita*
I'd like my steak rare/medium/well done	ステーキはレアー／ミーディアム／ウエルダンでお願いします *sutēki wa reā/midiamu/uerudan de o-negai shimasu*

Paying

- Just about everything in Japan is subject to consumption tax. This is not normally included in the price shown, but is added at the cash desk. It currently stands at about 3%.

Excuse me, will you bring the bill, please?	すみません、お勘定／お愛想してもらえますか *sumimasen. o-kanjō/o-aisō shite moraemasu ka*
Is service included?	サービス料は入っていますか *sābisu-ryō wa haitte imasu ka*
Is the cover charge included?	テーブルチャージは入っていますか *tēburu chāji wa haitte imasu ka*
Do you accept traveller's cheques?	トラベラーズチェックは使えますか *toraberāzu chekku wa tsukaemasu ka*
Have you got change?	小さいお金はありますか *chiisai o-kane wa arimasu ka*
Keep the change	お釣は取っておいて下さい *o-tsuri wa totte oite kudasai*
Is the consumption tax included?	消費税は入っていますか *shōhi-zei wa haitte imasu ka*
Is everything included?	全部入っていますか *zenbu haitte imasu ka*
Excuse me, there's a mistake	すみません、まちがいがありますが *sumimasen, machigai ga arimasu ga*
I/we had the fixed-price meal	私／私達は定食を食べました *watashi/watashi-tachi wa teishoku o tabemashita*

We had three bottles of . . .

私達は. . .を3本飲みました
watashi-tachi wa . . . o san-bon nomimashita

I had the steak

私はステーキを食べました
watashi wa sutēki o tabemashita

How much is that?

それはいくらですか
sore wa ikura desu ka

But you have put . . . yen on the bill (check)

でも、お勘定には. . .円と付いています
demo, o-kanjō niwa . . . en to tsuite imasu

You may hear:

サービス料は入っています *sābisu-ryō wa haitte imasu*	Service is included
サービス料は入っていません *sābisu-ryō wa haitte imasen*	Service isn't included
コーヒーはいかがですか *kōhī wa ikaga desu ka*	Would you like coffee?
デザートはいかがですか *dezāto wa ikaga desu ka*	Would you like a dessert?
ございません／切れています *gozaimasen/kirete imasu*	We don't have any
直ぐに変えて参ります *sugu ni kaete mairimasu*	I'll change it right away
お食事はいかがでしたか *o-shokuji wa ikaga deshita ka*	How was the meal?
どうも有難う御座いました *dōmo arigatō gozaimashita*	Thank you very much
又、どうぞ *mata dōzo*	Come again, please

Eating Out

I/we ordered...	私／私達は...を注文しました
	watashi/watashi-tachi wa . . . o chūmon shimashita
I/we didn't order...	私／私達は...は注文しませんでした
	watashi/watashi-tachi wa . . . wa chūmon shimasen deshita
You have put it on the bill	お勘定にはそれが付けてあります
	o-kanjō niwa sore ga tsukete arimasu
You are wrong	あなたは間違っています
	anata wa machigatte imasu
You are right	あなたの言う通りです
	anata no iu tōri desu

In the sushi shop

- This very popular and uniquely Japanese dish is really the one that the Japanese take most delight in. It's a dish they love to discuss and entertain their friends with. A sushi shop is usually a small, cramped restaurant with a glass, refrigerated counter full of fresh and raw fish, shellfish, eggs and vegetables. Most customers sit and eat at the counter. There are usually a small number of tables scattered around the shop. Fish, shell fish and vegetables are rolled up in, laid on, or mixed with a vinegary, sweet rice shaped into two bite-sized pieces. These pieces are dipped in soy sauce (usually by hand) before being eaten. What is different about the sushi shop though, is that the customer points to what they want to eat and it's served on a lacquer or wooden board immediately after preparation. Hot sake is a natural accompaniment to sushi in the winter months, cold draught beer in the summer. Don't miss this delightful experience.

Some common sushi dishes:

まぐろ（鮪） *maguro*	**raw tuna**
あなご *anago*	**sea eel**
はまち *hamachi*	**raw yellowtail**
たこ（蛸） *tako*	**boiled octopus**
とり貝 *torigai*	**raw cockles**
いか *ika*	**raw squid**
かに（蟹） *kani*	**boiled crab**
いくら *ikura*	**salmon roe**
えび（海老） *ebi*	**boiled prawn**
うに *uni*	**raw sea urchin**
鉄火巻 *tekka-maki*	**raw tuna roll**
穴胡巻 *anakyu-maki*	**cooked sea eel and cucumber roll**
しんこ巻 *shinko-maki*	**pickled radish roll**
とろ鉄火巻 *toro tekka maki*	**raw tuna roll**
にぎり盛合せ *nigiri moriawase*	**a mixture of sushi pieces usually served on a traditional wooden platter with sliced pickled ginger**

- To make these small parcels of food, a sushi chef (*itamae*) uses dry laver (a type of edible seaweed).

Charcoal grill shops

- *Robatayaki-ya* are great levellers in Japanese society, attracting people from all walks of life. Almost everybody likes to visit them. Again, there is a refrigerated counter display, often in the form of a large circle. The customers sit around the outside while the staff cook and serve from the inside. You choose from a huge variety of fresh fish, meat, shell fish, vegetables and the ubiquitous tofu dishes. They are then barbecued and served immediately.
- The best *robatas* are boisterous places and great fun to eat in if you can stand the noise. They usually fall into low–medium price ranges, with the whole range of beverages on offer. Sushi is sometimes served, but it is invariably an inferior product to the real thing found in the sushi shop.

Samples of Robatayaki dishes

海老焼 *ebi yaki*	barbecued prawn
鳥もも焼き *tori momo yaki*	barbecued chicken leg
あさりのバター煮 *asari no batā ni*	clams cooked in butter
じゃがいもバター *jagaimo batā*	baked potato with butter
冷奴 *hiyayakko*	cold blocks of tofu with chopped spring onions and dried fish flakes
たこ酢 *takosu*	boiled octopus in sugary vinegar fish stock
おでん *oden*	a hotchpotch stew with potatoes, whole eggs, soy bean curd, radish, fish cakes, squid etc
納豆 *nattō*	fermented soybean mixed with soy sauce, green onions and mustard

肉じゃが *niku jaga*	a beef stew with potatoes, cooked in soy sauce

Pancake shops

- The *okonomiyaki* has been described as a Japanese pancake. It uses a cabbage, flour and egg base with a variety of toppings and is usually very good value for money.
- These 'fast food' restaurants attract many students and younger Japanese.
- The pancakes are cooked on a large, hot, iron counter. The same restaurants also specialise in *yaki-soba* – fried buckwheat noodles – cooked in the same way.
- All the accoutrements are generally available: sake, shochu, beer, cola etc.
- *Teppan-yaki* dishes (thinly sliced beef and pork) are sometimes available at this type of restaurant, served with finely chopped raw cabbage and a bitter orange juice dip (*ponzu* ぽん酢).

Some typical *okonomiyaki* dishes:

お好み焼 *okonomiyaki*	pancake
豚お好み焼 *buta okonomiyaki*	pork pancake
いかお好み焼 *ika okonomiyaki*	squid pancake
焼そば *yaki-soba*	fried noodles
きも焼そば *kimo yaki-soba*	pork or chicken liver and noodles
ちゃんぽん焼そば *chanpon yaki-soba*	meat and shellfish mixture and noodles
オムそば *omu soba*	fried noodles wrapped in an omelette

Other dishes

The following Japanese dishes are to be found in
specialised restaurants and in the large international
hotels of Tokyo, Osaka, Yokohama etc.

Suki-yaki すきやき

Very thin slices of beef cooked in an iron pot,
usually at the table, with soya bean curd (tofu),
mushrooms, Chinese cabbage, leeks and carrots.
The dish includes a vermicelli made from a very
strange substance known as 'Devil's tongue' (*Kon
nyaku*).
A little sugar is used with soy sauce and sake. When
cooked, the ingredients are picked from the pan and
dipped in raw egg before eating.

Tenpura てんぷら (天麩羅)

Shellfish, fish and vegetables, deep fried in batter,
served with a dipping bowl containing *Dashi* (fish
stock), soy sauce and grated radish.
This dish is very popular with the foreign visitors to
Japan who are less adventurous eaters. The
ingredients contain few unknowns.
The Japanese tend to save this dish for special
occasions – often when they invite foreign guests
to dinner!

Shabu-shabu しゃぶしゃぶ

Thin slices of good quality beef, mushrooms, and
bean-curd are boiled in a matter of seconds in a pre-
prepared stock.
The mouth-watering slivers of beef are dipped in a
sauce containing *Dashi* and lemon juice.
There are restaurants specialising in this dish,
particularly in the Kobe area which boasts the finest
'beer-fed' beef in Japan. They can be very
expensive.

Chanko nabe ちゃんこなべ

- This is the food Sumo wrestlers eat, and is cooked in a very large pot.
- Chicken(s), fish (whole salmon are preferred) and a wide variety of vegetables are cooked together and served with large bowls of boiled rice and gallons of beer and sake.

Yaki-tori やきとり（焼鳥）

- Bite-size chunks of chicken, chicken livers and chicken gizzards are arranged on bamboo skewers with leeks, onions or peppers. Dipped in a sweet barbecue sauce, they are then broiled over a charcoal fire.
- Japan is bursting with *Yaki-tori* shops. They are very popular, but they are not always cheap eating, particularly if they are very specialised.

Drinks

Alcoholic drinks

- The Japanese consume more whisky（ウイスキー） per capita than any other nation in the world. However, the national drink is *sake* 酒 (rice wine), and the most popular drink in the country, particularly in the summertime, is beer.
- Sake is a colourless wine, made from rice, with an alcohol content of about 16%. It is usually drunk hot from small cups to accompany food. It is claimed that the best sake comes from Nada in Kobe (by the brewers of Nada, Kobe) but other cities, Kyoto and Hiroshima, for example, are centres of excellence.
- Japanese beer is of a high quality, although somewhat limited in variety – there are only four brewers in the whole country.
- Whisky and wines are imported in large quantities, though there is an increasing tendency for the Japanese to build more of their own distilleries and plant more vines.

Eating Out

Non-alcoholic beverages

Green tea is still the most popular non-alcoholic drink. There is a whole etiquette surrounding tea and a time-honoured way of serving it to your guests.

The tea ceremony (茶の湯 *Cha no yu,*) is a popular art form studied by many Japanese men and women. Like the martial arts, it is a skill only acquired through much practice, and many young women regard it as a necessary accomplishment for a wife to have.

Coffee is very popular and most coffee shops sell many kinds. Street vending machines sell cola, fruit juices and 'sports drinks' to the tune of some twenty billion cans a year.

'd like...	下さい *...kudasai*
...a bottle of beer/wine	ビール／ワイン1本 *biru/wain ip-pon...*
...a jug of beer	ジョッキ1杯 *jokki ip-pai...*
...a glass of beer/wine	ビール／ワイン1杯 *biru/wain ip-pai...*
ed wine	赤ワイン *aka wain*
vhite wine	白ワイン *shiro wain*
osé	ローゼ *rōze*
Iry sake	辛口の酒 *karakuchi no sake*
weet sake	甘口の酒 *amakuchi no sake*

Eating Out

whisky and water	ウイスキーの水割り *uisukī no mizuwari*
a brandy	ブランデー *burandē*
Tea, please	お茶を下さい *o-cha o kudasai*
Two cups of coffee, please	コーヒー2つ下さい *Kōhi futatsu kudasai*
Some juice, please	ジュースを下さい *jūsu o kudasai*

ENTERTAINMENT AND SPORT

Sport is very important to the Japanese, with fitness and health being a national obsession. Millions of youngsters play baseball at school and then go on to play at college, university and often for their company too.

Sumo (相撲) is the national spectator sport with grand champions amassing huge fortunes, only to die an early death through heart failure and diabetes.

The martial arts are as popular as ever. Judo (柔道) Karate (空手) and Aikido (合気道) clubs proliferate, and Kendo (剣道) is practised in secondary schools up and down the country.

Tennis and swimming are popular summer sports, and many hotels have their own pools and courts. Check with the Tourist Information Centre.

Cycling is on the increase as a popular pastime, and

many cycle tracks are being built separately from the main road. Pick your routes carefully though. The unwary cyclist can spend hours puffing and blowing up some very steep roads wishing they were elsewhere. Japan is a very mountainous country.

At the cinema or theatre

- The three best known forms of traditional Japanese theatre are *Noh* (能) from the 14th century, *Kabuki* (歌舞伎) and *Bunraku* (文楽) from the 17th century. Noh was traditional entertainment for the Samurai, whereas Kabuki and Bunraku had more popular appeal among the commoners. The latter forms are still more popular today. All three provide a glimpse into Japanese history in that each type of theatre reaches its audience in its original form.
- Noh is characterised by the uniqueness of its masks, slow dance movements and *utai*, a strange evocative chant.
- Kabuki has a wider appeal than Noh. Performed exclusively by men, there is a strong folk appeal where music and dancing are fundamental. The use of a revolving stage in order to change sets and costumes very quickly is a surprising feature.
- Bunraku is Japan's puppet theatre. It is still quite popular, especially in the Osaka area.
- Theatre performances, prices, dates etc are available through the Tourist Information Centre.

What's on at the cinema?	どんな映画が上映されていますか *donna eiga ga jōei sarete imasu ka*
What's on at the theatre?	どんな芝居／演劇が上演されていますか *donna shibai/engeki ga jōen sarete imasu ka*

Entertainment and Sport

Is it . . . ?	（それは）...ですか *(sore wa)...desu ka*
. . . an American film	アメリカ映画 *. . . amerika eiga . . .*
. . . a cartoon	漫画（まんが） *. . . manga . . .*
. . . a comedy	喜劇／喜劇映画 *. . . kigeki/kigeki eiga . . .*
. . . a detective film	探偵映画／刑事映画 *. . . tantei eiga/keiji eiga . . .*
. . . a documentary	ドキュメンタリー／記録 映画 *. . . dokyumentarī/kiroku* *eiga . . .*
. . . a gangster film	やくざ映画 *. . . yakuza eiga . . .*
. . . a romance	恋愛物語／冒険物語 *. . . ren'ai monogatari/bōken* *monogatari . . .*
. . . a tragedy	悲劇／悲劇映画 *. . . higeki/higeki eiga . . .*
. . . a western	西部劇／西部物 *. . . seibu-geki/seibu-* *mono . . .*
. . . Kabuki	歌舞伎 *. . . kabuki . . .*
. . . Bunraku	文楽 *. . . bunraku . . .*
. . . a Noh play	能 *. . . nō . . .*
. . . a musical	ミュージカル *. . . myūjikaru . . .*

Is the film newly released?

その映画は最近封切られましたか

sono eiga wa saikin fūgiraremashita ka

Is the film . . . ?

その映画は . . . ですか

sono eiga wa . . . desu ka

. . . in black and white

白黒

. . . shiro-kuro . . .

. . . in colour

カラー

. . . karā . . .

. . . in English

英語版

. . . eigo-ban . . .

Is the film dubbed?

その映画は吹き替えになっていますか

sono eiga wa fukikae ni natte imasu ka

Is the film with the original soundtrack?

その映画にはオリジナルのサウンドトラックがついていますか

sono eiga niwa orijinaru no saundo-torakku ga tsuite imasu ka

Are there sub-titles?

見出しがついていますか

midashi ga tsuite imasu ka

Who's in it?

誰が出演していますか

dare ga shutsuen shite imasu ka

How much is a seat . . . ?

席はいくらですか。

. . . seki wa ikura desu ka

. . . in the balcony

二階桟敷の

ni-kai sajiki no . . .

. . . in the stalls

一階前方の

ik-kai zenpō no . . .

Entertainment and Sport

. . . near the stage	舞台近くの *butai chikaku no . . .*
. . . for an adult/a child	大人の／子供の *otona no/kodomo no . . .*
Is there a special discount price . . . ?	割引料金はありますか *. . . waribiki-ryōkin wa arimasu ka*
. . . for children	子供用の *kodomo yō no . . .*
. . . for a group	団体用の *dantai yō no . . .*
. . . for students	学生用の *gakusei yō no . . .*

Booking

I'd like . . .	お願いします *. . . o-negai shimasu*
. . . two seats in the stalls	一階最前列の席を二枚 *ik-kai sai-zenretsu no seki o ni-mai . . .*
. . . four seats together in the stalls	一階最前列で一緒に座れる席を四枚 *ik-kai sai-zenretsu de issho ni suwareru seki o yon-mai . . .*
. . . a seat not too far back	あまり後過ぎない席を一枚 *amari ushiro suginai seki o ichi-mai . . . . . .*
. . . a seat in the middle	真ん中の席を一枚 *mannaka no seki o ichi-mai . . .*
. . . a ticket for the afternoon performance	午後の興行の切符を一枚 *gogo no kōgyō no kippu o ichi-mai . . .*

Times

At what time does . . . begin?	は何時に始まりますか *. . . wa nan-ji ni hajimarimasu ka*
At what time does . . . end?	は何時に終わりますか *. . . wa nan-ji ni owarimasu ka*

. . . the afternoon performance . . .	午後の興行／午後の芝居 *. . . gogo no kōgyō/gogo no shibai*
. . . the first performance . . .	最初の興行／最初の芝居 *. . . saisho no kōgyō/saisho no shibai*
. . . the last performance . . .	最後の興行／最後の芝居 *. . . saigo no kōgyō/ saigo no shibai*
. . . the interval . . .	幕間／休憩時間 *. . . makuai/kyūkei jikan*

Has the Kabuki performance begun?	歌舞伎の興行は始まりましたか *kabuki no kōgyō wa hajimarimashita ka*
Can we order drinks in the interval?	幕間／休憩時間に飲み物を注文してもいいですか *makuai/kyūkei jikan ni nomimono o chūmon shite mo ii desu ka*
Is there a Bunraku matinee performance?	文楽の昼興行はありますか *bunraku no hiru kōgyō wa arimasu ka*
Is there a cloakroom?	外套類／携帯品　預り所はありますか *gaitō-rui/keitai-hin azukari-jo wa arimasu ka*

Opinions

What did you think of it?	それについてどう思いましたか *sore ni tsuite dō omoimashita ka*
It was awful	ひどかったです *hidokatta desu*
It was boring	うんざりしました／退屈でした *unzari shimashita/taikutsu deshita*
It was fantastic	素晴らしかったです *subarashikatta desu*
It was frightening	恐ろしかったです *osoroshikatta desu*
It was funny	面白かったです *omoshirokatta desu*
I found it very interesting	私には非常に興味がありました *watashi niwa hijō ni kyōmi ga arimashita*

You may hear:	
禁煙です **kin'en desu**	Smoking not allowed
禁止されています／許可されていません **kinshi sarete imasu/kyoka sarete imasen**	It is not allowed
切符を拝見します **kippu o haiken shimasu**	Your ticket, please
プログラムご入用の方はこちらへどうぞ **puroguramu o go-nyūyō no kata wa kochira e dōzo**	This way please for a programme

Other entertainments

Is/are there . . . near here?	この近くに...はありますか *kono chikaku ni . . . wa* *arimasu ka*
Is/are there . . . in the town?	この町に...はありますか *kono machi ni . . . wa* *arimasu ka*

. . . a baseball ground . . .	野球場 *. . . yakyū-jō . . .*
. . . a castle . . .	お城 *. . . o-shiro . . .*
. . . a famous place for cherry blossom viewing . . .	花見の名所 *. . . hana-mi no meisho . . .*
. . . a Japanese fencing hall	剣道の道場 *. . . kendō no dōjō . . .*
. . . a Judo hall . . .	柔道の道場 *. . . jūdō no dōjō . . .*
. . . a Karate hall . . .	空手の道場 *. . . karate no dōjō . . .*
. . . a hot spring . . .	温泉 *. . . onsen . . .*
. . . a shrine . . .	神社 *. . . jinja . . .*
. . . a temple . . .	お寺／仏閣 *. . . o-tera/bukkaku . . .*
. . . a fun fair . . .	遊園地 *. . . yūenchi . . .*
. . . a path up the mountain . . .	登山路 *. . . tozan-michi . . .*
. . . a tennis court . . .	テニスコート *. . . tenisu-kōto . . .*
. . . an indoor swimming pool . . .	室内プール *. . . shitsunai pūru . . .*

. . . an outdoor swimming pool . . .	屋外プール . . . *okugai pūru* . . .
. . . a heated swimming pool	温水プール . . . *onsui pūru* . . .
. . . a skating rink . . .	スケート場 . . . *sukēto-jō* . . .
. . . skiing ground . . .	スキー場 . . . *sukī-jō* . . .
. . . a golf course . . .	ゴルフ場 . . . *gorufu-jō* . . .
. . . a lake . . .	湖 . . . *mizuumi* . . .
. . . any walks . . .	散歩道 . . . *sanpo-michi* . . .
. . . a concert hall . . .	コンサートホール . . . *konsāto hōru* . . .
. . . a bathing resort . . .	海水浴場 . . . *kaisui-yoku-jō* . . .

Where can I see . . . ?	どこで . . . が見れますか *doko de . . . ga miremasu ka*

. . . a baseball game	野球の試合 . . . *yakyū no shiai* . . .
. . . a football (soccer) match	フットボール（サッカー） の試合 . . . *futto-bōru (sakkā) no shiai* . . .
. . . sumo wrestling	相撲の取組み . . . *sumō no torikumi* . . .
. . . Japanese fencing/Judo/ Karate/Aikido match	剣道／柔道／空手／ 合気道の試合 . . . *kendō/jūdō/karate/ aikidō no shiai* . . .
. . . a festival	お祭り . . . *o-matsuri* . . .

57

. . .a yacht race   ヨットレース
                          . . .yotto rēsu. . .

. . .horse racing   競馬
                          . . .keiba. . .

. . .bicycle racing   競輪
                          . . .keirin. . .

Sumo

- Sumo is Japan's national sport, but largely for spectators. There are just six tournaments (大相撲 *o-zumo*) every year, each lasting 15 days.
  The wrestlers fight bare-handed and wear only a loin-cloth (回し *mawashi*).
  Before the actual fight commences, a set of rituals are gone through – foot-stamping, face wiping, salt-throwing (to purify the ring) – and millions of eyes are glued religiously to NHK TV. When battle has commenced, the first wrestler to touch the ground with any part of his body other than the soles of his feet or to be pushed out of the ring is the loser.
- Sumo champions (横綱 *Yokozuna*) are regarded as national heroes in Japan. Don't be misled by the shape of these wrestlers. They are extremely fit and agile athletes. There is no sham involved in the 2000 year old sport.
- The wrestlers (関取 *sekitori*) have huge followings and Sumo groupies visit all the tournaments in large numbers.

Skiing

skates   スケート靴
                          sukēto gutsu

ski boots   スキー靴
                          sukī gutsu

ski equipment   スキー用具
                          sukī yōgu

kis	スキー *sukī*
ki pants	スキーズボン *sukī zubon*
ki lift	リフト *rifuto*
ki jumping	スキージャンプ *sukī janpu*
ki suits	スキー服 *sukī fuku*
ki slopes	スロープ *surōpu*
ki running	スキー滑走 *sukī kassō*
skiing ground	スキー場 *sukī-jō*
ki sticks	スキー用ストック *sukī yō sutokku*
ki instructor	スキーの指導員 *sukī no shidō-in*
skier	スキーヤー *sukīyā*
sledge	そり *sori*
indings	ビンディング *bindingu*
o ski	スキーをする *sukī o suru*
kiing lessons	スキーのレッスン *sukī no ressun*

Visiting a town

Where is...?	はどこですか ...wa doko desu ka
...the tourist information centre	旅行案内所 ryokō annai-jo...
...the castle	お城 o-shiro...
...the church	教会 kyōkai...
...the market	市場 ichiba...
...the museum	博物館 hakubutsu-kan...
...the shrine	神社 jinja...
...the temple	お寺／仏閣 o-tera/bukkaku...
...the shopping centre	商店街 shōten-gai...

Is it open on Sundays?	日曜日はあいていますか nichiyōbi wa aite imasu ka
Can I take photos?	写真を撮ってもいいですか shashin o tottemo ii desu ka
Do you have a guide book in English?	英語のガイドブックを持っ いますか eigo no gaido bukku o mott imasu ka
Is there a guided tour?	ガイド付き旅行はあります gaido tsuki ryokō wa arimasu ka
Do you have any picture postcards?	絵はがきはありますか e-hagaki wa arimasu ka

Meeting people

You should take your coat off before entering the hallway. Once inside, you should take your shoes off and place them with the rest of the family's shoes. You will be offered slippers to wear.
Bowing is much more common than shaking hands, and can be used for exchanging greetings, thanking someone, saying goodbye and apologising. You should shake hands only if your host offers his or her hand.
It is extremely useful to have your 'name card' (*meishi*) printed. These are used much more than our business cards, in social as well as commercial situations.
Almost all Japanese homes have the name of the head of the household printed on a small plaque beside the front door.

What's your name?	お名前は何ですか *o-namae wa nan desu ka*
My name is...	私の名前は...です *watashi no namae* *wa...desu*
Pleased to meet you	どうぞ宜しく *dōzo yoroshiku*
Is this seat free?	この席はあいていますか *kono seki wa aite imasu ka*
Do you mind if I smoke?	煙草を吸っても構いませんか *tabako o suttemo* *kamaimasen ka*
Do you have a lighter/a box of matches?	ライター／マッチを持ってい ますか *raitā/matchi o motte imasu* *ka*
Would you like to have something to eat/drink?	食べ物／飲み物はいかがです か *tabemono/nomimono wa* *ikaga desu ka*

I'm with my...	と一緒です *...to issho desu*
...family	家族 *kazoku...*
...friends	友達／友人 *tomodachi/yūjin...*
...boy friend(s)	ボーイフレンド／男友達 *bōi furendo/otoko* *tomodachi...*
...girl friend(s)	ガールフレンド／女友達 *gāru furendo/onna* *tomodachi...*
...husband	主人 *shujin...*
...wife	妻／かなえ *tsuma/kanae...*
Where are you from?	どちらから見えましたか／出身 はどちらですか *dochira kara miemashita* *ka/shusshin wa dochira des* *ka*
I'm from Kobe	神戸です *Kōbe desu*
I'm on holiday	私は休暇中です *watashi wa kyūka-chū desu*
I'm studying here	ここで勉強しています *koko de benkyō shite imasu*
I'm here on business	仕事でここに来ています *shigoto de koko ni kite* *imasu*
What do you do?	何をなさってますか *nani o nasattemasu ka*
What are you studying?	何を勉強していますか *nani o benkyō shite imasu k*

How long have you been living here?	どの位ここに住んでおられますか *dono kurai koko ni sunde oraremasu ka*
How is your family?	ご家族の皆さんはお元気ですか *go-kazoku no mina-san wa o-genki desu ka*
Which company do you work for?	どの会社にお勤めですか *dono kaisha ni o-tsutome desu ka*

Reactions

It's...	(それは)...です *(sore wa)...desu*
..wonderful/great	素晴らしい *...subarashii...*
..(very) beautiful	(とても) 美しい *...(totemo) utsukushii...*
..interesting	おもしろい／興味深い *...omoshiroi/kyōmi bukai...*
..horrible	ひどい *...hidoi...*

Business expressions

I'm (Mr/Mrs/Miss) Smith	私はスミスです *watashi wa Sumisu desu*
I'm from JCCL	私は JCCL の者です *watashi wa jei-shī-shī eru no mono desu*
I'm (Mr) Tanaka from JCCL	私は JCCL の田中です *watashi wa jei-shī-shī eru no Tanaka desu*

63

I have an appointment with...	私は...と会うことになっています *watashi wa...to au koto ni natte imasu*
...Mr/Mrs/Miss Suzuki	鈴木さん *...Suzuki-san...*
...my customers	お客さん *...o-kyaku-san...*
Is your sales manager, Mr Kobayashi, in?	販売課長の小林さんはおられますか *hanbai kachō no Kobayashi-san wa oraremasu ka*
Can I speak to...?	をお願いします *...o o-negai shimasu*
...your personnel manager	人事課長さん *jinji kachō san...*
...your general manager, Mr Kondo	近藤部長さん *Kondō buchō san...*
...somebody in the business department	営業部のどなたか *eigyō-bu no donata ka...*
Here is my card	名刺をどうぞ *meishi o dōzo*
I'm sorry I'm late	遅れてすみません *okurete sumimasen*
I'm in the hotel...	ホテルにいます *...hoteru ni imasu*
...tonight	今夜 *konya...*
...till 10 o'clock in the morning	明日の朝、十時まで *asu no asa, jū-ji made...*

HEALTH

Check that you have sufficient medical insurance
and that it is valid in Japan. If you have a particular
medical condition, you should ensure that the
condition is written in Japanese, and you should
carry a card holding that information at all times.
Whenever possible, take your own medication with
you, as many Japanese medications are unsuitable
for the Caucasian metabolism. (Drug strengths
tend to be lower, due to the lower average weight
of a Japanese person.)

Drugs are dispensed by the physician at his surgery
or at a hospital pharmacy. If you are taking
medication on a regular basis, ensure that you have
sufficient supplies for your stay in Japan.

You should ensure that you get a receipt for any
treatment you receive, as you will need it to claim
on your medical insurance.

Complaints and conditions

I have diarrhoea	下痢をしています *geri o shite imasu*
I have flu	インフルエンザに　かかって います *infuruenza ni kakatte imasu*
I am allergic to antibiotics/penicillin	抗生物質／ペニシリンに対 アレルギーです *kōsei-busshitsu/penishirin n taishi arerugi desu*
I have twisted my ankle	足首を捻挫しました *ashi-kubi o nenza shimashita*
I have dizzy spells	ちょっと　眩暈がします *chotto memai ga shimasu*
I am epileptic	癲癇にかかっています *tenkan ni kakatte imasu*
I have a heart problem	心臓病に　かかっています *shinzō-byō ni kakatte imasu*
I have high blood pressure	高血圧症にかかっています *koketsuatsu-shō ni kakatte imasu*
I feel shivery	悪寒がします／ぞくぞくし す *okan ga shimasu/zoku-zoku shimasu*
I have been stung by . . .	に刺されました *. . . ni sasaremashita*
. . . a bee/wasp	蜜蜂／蜂 *mitsubachi/hachi . . .*
. . . an ant	蟻 *ari . . .*
. . . a mosquito	蚊 *ka . . .*

Health

. . . an insect	虫 *mushi . . .*
My . . . hurts	が痛いです *. . . ga itai desu*
. . . arm	腕 *ude . . .*
. . . back	背中 *senaka . . .*
. . . chest	胸 *mune . . .*
. . . eyes	目 *me . . .*
. . . head	頭 *atama . . .*
. . . leg	足 *ashi . . .*
. . . stomach	胃／腹部 *i/fukubu . . .*
. . . tooth	歯 *ha . . .*
I have period pains	生理痛があります *seiri-tsū ga arimasu*
I have asthma	喘息にかかっています *zensoku ni kakatte imasu*
I am airsick	飛行機に酔いました *hikōki ni yoimashita*
I am carsick	乗物に酔いました *norimono ni yoimashita*

You may hear:

を あげます **...o agemasu**	I'm going to give you...
この クリーム **kono kurīmu**	this cream
この薬 **kono kusuri**	this medicine
この処方箋 **kono shohō-sen**	this prescription
この経口避妊薬 **kono keikō hinin-yaku**	these pills
注射をします **chūsha o shimasu**	I'm going to give you an injection
すぐに横になって休んでください **sugu ni yoko ni natte yasunde kudasai**	Go to bed straight away
三日間寝ていて下さい **mik-kakan nete ite kudasai**	Stay in bed for three days
どうしましたか **dō shimashita ka**	What's the matter?
どこが痛いですか **doko ga itai desu ka**	Where does it hurt?
この薬を...飲んで下さい **kono kusuri o...nonde kudasai**	You must take this medicine...
一日三回 **...ichi-nichi san-kai...**	...three times a day
一回二錠 **...ik-kai ni-jō**	...two tablets at a time
食前／食後に **...shoku-zen/shoku-go ni...**	...before meals/after meals

Health

I have a cold	風邪を引いています *kaze o hiite imasu*
I am constipated	便秘をしています *benpi o shite imasu*
I am diabetic	糖尿病にかかっています *tonyōbyō ni kakatte imasu*
I feel sick	気分が悪いです *kibun ga warui desu*
I have a sore throat	喉が痛いです *nodo ga itai desu*

I've been in pain...	痛みがあります *...itami ga arimasu*

...for a week	一週間 *is-shūkan...*
...for three days	三日間 *mik-kakan...*
...since yesterday	昨日から *kinō kara...*
...since this morning	今朝から *kesa kara...*
...for a few hours	数時間 *sū-jikan...*

I had the same problem...	同じ病気にかかりました *...onaji byoki ni kakarimashita*

...last year	昨年 *sakunen...*
...a few years ago	数年前（に） *sū-nen mae (ni)...*
...two months ago	二か月前（に） *ni-kagetsu mae (ni)...*

At the dentist's

I have an awful toothache
ひどく歯が痛みます
hidoku ha ga itamimasu

When is the next available appointment?
次の予約はいつですか
tsugi no yoyaku wa itsu desu ka

When are your surgery hours?
診療時間は何時ですか
shinryō-jikan wa nan-ji desu ka

You may hear:

どうしましたか
dō shimashita ka
What's the matter?

痛みますか
itamimasu ka
Are you in pain?

今日の午後診療があります
kyō no gogo shinryō ga arimasu
There is a surgery this afternoon

応急措置をしますので二時に来てください
ōkyū-sochi o shimasu node, ni-ji ni kite kudasai
We will give you some emergency treatment, come here at 2 o'clock

お名前は何ですか
o-namae wa nan desu ka
What's your name?

虫歯の穴があります
mushi-ba no ana ga arimasu
There is a cavity in your tooth

歯を抜きます
ha o nukimasu
I'm going to extract your tooth

次回、来院時にこの診察券を持参してください
jikai, raiin-ji ni kono shinsatsu-ken o jisan shite kudasai
When you visit the surgery next time, bring this consultation ticket with you

At the chemist's shop

I would like...	を お願いします *...o o-negai shimasu*

...some antiseptic cream	消毒用クリーム *shōdoku-yō kurīmu...*
...some aspirin	アスピリン *asupirin...*
...a bandage	包帯 *hōtai...*
...some cotton wool	脱脂綿 *dasshi-men...*
...some medicine for the stomach and bowels	胃腸薬 *ichō-yaku...*
...some medicine for a cold	風邪薬 *kaze-gusuri...*
...a sticking plaster	絆創膏 *bansō kō...*
...some eye lotion	目薬 *me-gusuri*
...sanitary towels	生理用ナプキン *seiri-yō napukin...*
...some tampons	タンポン *tanpon*
...something for insect bites	虫刺されに効く薬 *mushi-sasare ni kiku kusuri...*

Where is the nearest chemist's shop?	最寄りの薬屋／薬局はどこですか *moyori no kusuri-ya/ yakkyoku wa doko desu ka*
What time does the chemist's shop open?	薬屋／薬局は何時に開きますか *kusuri-ya/yakkyoku wa nan-ji ni akimasu ka*

At the optician's

I've broken my glasses	眼鏡がこわれました *megane ga kowaremashita*
Can you repair them?	修理して頂けますか *shūri shite itadakemasu ka*
How much does it cost?	いくらかかりますか *ikura kakarimasu ka*
When will they be ready?	いつ出来上がりますか *itsu dekiagarimasu ka*
I've lost one of my contact lenses	片方のコンタクトレンズを失くしました *katahō no kontakuto-renzu o nakushimashita*
I wear hard/soft contact lenses	ハード／ソフトのコンタクトレンズをしています *hādo/sofuto no kontakuto-renzu o shite imasu*
I'm short-sighted/long-sighted	私は近視／遠視です *watashi wa kinshi/enshi desu*
I want a pair of sunglasses, too	サングラスも欲しいのですが、 *sangurasu mo hoshii no desu ga*

You may hear:

視力を検査します
shiryoku o kensa shimasu

I'm going to test your eyesight

どちらのコンタクトレンズをしていますかハードですかソフトですか。
dochira no kontakuto-renzu o shite imasu ka, hādo desu ka sofuto desu ka

Which contact lenses do you wear, hard or soft?

TRAVEL

- There are two Tourist Information Centres (TIC) in Tokyo: one at Narita Airport and the other close to Yurakucho JR (Japan Railways) station in Tokyo city. There is a third TIC close to Kyoto JR station to cater for those people entering Japan at Osaka International airport. The TIC provides maps and guides written in English and plenty of information about places of interest.
- You can also obtain information prior to your visit by contacting the Japan National Tourist Organisation which has offices worldwide. The London office is located at 167 Regent Street, London W1 (071-734 9638).
- Whilst you are in the airport you should obtain your JR Pass with an exchange voucher This can be done at the JR ticket counter. Remember, if you intend to use JR trains, you must get your exchange voucher before you leave for Japan.

Travel

- Domestic Airlines provide an extensive network of flights at competitive fares, making this a popular way to travel around Japan for those who might be a little pushed for time.
- Travel by car isn't really recommended in the large cities, as public transport is generally very good. However, once you get into the countryside, a car can get you to places you might not otherwise see. The Japanese drive on the left.
- Hitch-hiking is not particularly popular as a means of getting about, but it's not illegal and presents little difficulty. Be prepared to talk to the journey's end with the driver, who will want to practise his or her English – it's for that reason you were picked up in the first place.

Travel by bus

Where is the bus stop for...?	行きのバスの停留所(バス停) はどこですか ...iki no basu no teiryū-jo wa doko desu ka
Which bus number should I take to get to...?	へ行くには何番のバスに乗ればいいですか ...e iku niwa nan-ban no basu ni noreba ii desu ka
What time does the bus leave?	そのバスは何時こ出ますか sono basu wa nan-ji ni demasu ka
How often does the bus leave for...?	行きのバスは何分置きに出ますか ...iki no basu wa nan-pun oki ni demasu ka
Do I need to change buses?	バスを乗り換えなければなりませんか basu o norikaenakereba narimasen ka
I want to go to...Where should I get off?	へ行きたいんですが。どこで降りたらいいですか ...e ikitai n desu ga. doko de oritara ii desu ka

How long does it take to get to . . .?	へはどの位かかりますか . . . ewa dono kurai kakarimasu ka
How far is it?	そこまでどの位の距離がありますか soko made dono kurai no kyori ga arimasu ka
Where is the ticket office for the bus?	バスの切符売場はどこですか basu no kippu uriba wa doko desu ka
How much is a single ticket/a return ticket to . . .?	まで片道／往復でいくらですか . . . made katamichi/ōfuku de ikura desu ka
Can I have two single tickets to . . .?	まで片道（切符）2枚お願いします . . . made katamichi (kippu) ni-mai o-negai shimasu
Can I have three return tickets to . . .?	まで往復（切符）3枚お願いします . . . made ōfuku (kippu) san-mai o-negai shimasu
Does this bus go to the city centre?	このバスは都心に行きますか kono basu wa toshin ni ikimasu ka
Please tell me when we get there	そこに着いたら教えて下さい soko ni tsuitara oshiete kudasai
I'd like a leaflet about bus excursions, please	バス周遊のリーフレットを下さい basu shūyū no rifuretto o kudasai
Is there a bus station near here?	この辺にバスの停留所はありますか kono hen ni basu no teiryū-jo wa arimasu ka
Can I have a book of tickets?	回数券を下さい kaisū-ken o kudasai

75

Is there a bus for Kyoto tomorrow?	明日、京都行きのバスはありますか *asu Kyōto iki no basu wa arimasu ka*
What time do we arrive in Osaka?	何時に大阪に着きますか *nan-ji ni Ōsaka ni tsukimasu ka*

Travel by taxi

Where can I find a taxi?	どこに行けばタクシーが見かりますか *doko ni ikeba takushī ga mitsukarimasu ka*
I want to go to. . .	へ行きたいんですが *. . .e ikitai n desu ga*
. . .the airport	空港 *kūkō. . .*
. . .the nearest underground	最寄りの地下鉄 *moyori no chikatetsu. . .*
. . .the Otani Hotel	大谷ホテル *Ōtani hoteru. . .*
. . .the JR station	国鉄の駅 *kokutetsu no eki. . .*
Where is the taxi stand?	タクシーのりばはどこですか *takushī noriba wa doko de ka*
How much is the fare?	料金はいくらですか *ryōkin wa ikura desu ka*
Will you go faster please?	もっと急いでくれますか *motto isoide kuremasu ka*
I have an important meeting	重要な会議があるので *jūyō na kaigi ga aru node*

How long will it take to get there by taxi?	タクシーでどの位かかりますか *takushi de dono kurai kakarimasu ka*
Can you take the motorway?	高速（道路）にのって下さい *kōsoku ni notte kudasai*
Will you slow down please?	もっとゆっくり行ってくれますか *motto yukkuri itte kuremasu ka*
It's near here	この近くです *kono chikaku desu*
Can you stop here?	ここで止めて下さい *koko de tomete kudasai*
Can you ask someone how to get there?	誰かに道をきいて貰えますか *dareka ni michi o kiite moraemasu ka*
Can I have a receipt, please?	領収書を貰えますか *ryōshū-sho o moraemasu ka*

You may see:

タクシーのりば（乗り場） ***takushi noriba***	taxi stand
個人タクシー ***kojin takushi***	private taxi
空車 ***kūsha***	for hire/vacant
割増 ***warimashi***	extra charge

Will you carry my bags?	鞄を運んで貰えますか *(kaban) o hakonde moraemasu ka*
Will you wait for me?	待っていて下さい *matte ite kudasai*

77

Travel

Travel by car

- All road signs are in Japanese once outside the built-up areas. You'll need an International Driver Permit, but hire rates are reasonable. Petrol is expensive.
- Don't drink and drive, as it's a very serious offence in Japan. You would run the risk of imprisonment
- Drive cautiously, because many pedestrians and cyclists don't observe the rules of the road. On top of this, such is the increase in the number of vehicles on the roads, it seems as though the whole country is a huge nursery for learner drivers with all the consequent hazards. The roads often have no pavements, and are used as play areas by children, so you have to keep a very watchful eye when driving about.
- Speed limits off the expressway are about 45 km/h but you will find that most drivers ignore this.
- Pedestrians always have the right of way, and accidents involving pedestrians will always be resolved in favour of the pedestrian regardless of circumstances. When you have to deal with the police in either an accident or a traffic offence the important thing is to stay cool and adopt an attitude of humility. It will be taken as sincerity or your part.

Car rental

Where can I rent a car?	どこでレンタカーが借りられますか *doko de renta-kā ga kariraremasu ka*
I'd like to hire a car	車を一台借りたいんですが *kuruma o ichi-dai karitai n desu ga*
large sized car/middle sized car/small sized car	大型車／中型車／小型車 *ōgata-sha/chūgata-sha/kogata-sha*

78

or two/four people	二人乗りの／四人乗りの *futari nori no/yo-nin nori no*
or a day/a week	一日／一週間 *ichi-nichi/is-shūkan*
What are your charges per ay/per kilometre?	一日／1キロメートルに付き いくらですか *ichi-nichi/ichi-kiro mētoru ni tsuki ikura desu ka*
How much is the deposit?	手付金はいくらですか *tetsuki-kin wa ikura desu ka*
Will you write it down, lease?	記入して頂けますか *kinyū shite itadakemasu ka*
What is the total cost?	全部でいくらですか *zenbu de ikura desu ka*

You may see:

駐車禁止 *chūsha-kinshi*	No parking
行き止まり *iki-domari*	Dead end
通行止 *tsūkō-dome*	Road closed
左側通行 *hidari gawa tsūkō*	Keep to the left
片側通行止 *katagawa tsūkō-dome*	One-way traffic
諸車通行止 *shosha tsūkō-dome*	Closed to all vehicles
無断立入を禁ず *mudan tachiiri o kinzu*	Unauthorized entry is forbidden
一方通行 *ippō tsūkō*	One-way traffic

You may hear:

運転免許証をお持ちですか
unten menkyo-shō o o-mochi desu ka
Do you have your driving license?

車はどの位ご入用ですか
kuruma wa dono kurai go-nyūyō desu ka
How long do you need a car?

これに記入して下さい
kore ni kinyū shite kudasai
Can you fill it in, please?

ここにサインして下さい
koko ni sain shite kudasai
Sign here, please

At a garage or petrol station

Where is the nearest petrol station?
最寄りのガソリンスタンドはどこですか
moyori no gasorin-sutando wa doko desu ka

Do you accept credit cards?
クレジットカードは使えますか
kurejitto-kādo wa tsukaemasu ka

Fill the tank, please
満タンにして下さい
man-tan ni shite kudasai

Give me . . . litres of standard/super/unleaded petrol, please
スタンダード／スーパー／鉛を . . . リットル入れて下さい
sutandādo/sūpā/muen o . . . rittoru irete kudasai

Give me . . . yen worth of standard/super/unleaded petrol, please
スタンダード／スーパー／鉛を . . . 円分入れて下さい
sutandādo/sūpā/muen o . . . en bun irete kudasai

How much is it a litre?
1リットルはいくらですか
ichi-rittoru wa ikura desu ka

I'll have the standard/super/unleaded, please
スタンダード／スーパー／鉛をにします
sutandādo/sūpā/muen o o-negai shimasu

Travel

Will you check the oil too?	オイルも点検して貰えますか *oiru mo tenken shite moraemasu ka*
Have you a road map?	道路地図はありますか *dōro chizu wa arimasu ka*
How much is that?	いくらですか *ikura desu ka*
How far is it to the motorway?	高速道路までどの位あります か *kōsoku dōro made dono kurai arimasu ka*
How far is the nearest town?	最寄りの町までどの位ありま すか *moyori no machi made dono kurai arimasu ka*
May we use the toilets?	トイレを借りてもいいですか *toire o karite mo ii desu ka*
Can I have some water?	水を貰えますか *mizu o moraemasu ka*
Can you put some air in the tyres?	タイヤに空気を入れて貰えま すか *taiya ni kūki o irete moraemasu ka*
I'd like a litre of oil	オイルを1リットル下さい *oiru o ichi-rittoru kudasai*

Will you check...?	を調べて貰えますか *...o shirabete moraemasu ka*

...the brakes	ブレーキ *burēki...*
...the oil	オイル *oiru...*
...the tyres	タイヤ *taiya...*

Travel

. . . the spare tyre	スペアタイヤ *supea taiya* . . .
. . . the water	水 *mizu* . . .
. . . the tyre pressure	タイヤ圧 *taiya-atsu* . . .
. . . the engine	エンジン *enjin* . . .

You may hear:

まっすぐ行って下さい **massugu itte kudasai**	Go straight on, please
ここから100メートル離れた所にあります **koko kara hyaku-metoru hanareta tokoro ni arimasu**	It's 100 metres from here
あそこです **asoko desu**	It's over there
レギュラーかプリミアム、どちらにしますか **regyurā ka primiamu dochira ni shimasu ka**	Do you want 2 or 4 star (regular or premium)?
プリミアムは1リットルにき . . . 円です **primiamu wa ichi-rittoru ni tsuki . . . yen desu**	4 star (premium) is . . . yen a litre
それでいいですか **sore de ii desu ka**	Is that all?
あそこで清算して下さい **asoko de seisan shite kudasai**	Please pay over there
その作りのものはありません **sono tsukuri no mono wa arimasen**	We haven't got any for that make
キー／鍵をお願いします **kī/kagi o o-negai shimasu**	May I have the key, please?

attendant	係員／案内係
	kakari-in/annai-gakari
cash desk	お勘定場
	o-kanjō-ba

Breakdowns and accidents

The car is near the JR Osaka/Kyoto/Kobe station	車は大阪／京都／神戸駅の近くにあります
	kuruma wa Ōsaka/Kyōto/Kōbe eki no chikaku ni arimasu
I've run out of petrol	ガソリンが切れました
	gasorin ga kiremashita
I've got a puncture (flat)	パンクしました
	panku shimashita
I was rammed by...	が衝突してきました
	...ga shōtotsu shite kimashita
I bumped into...	にぶつかりました
	...ni butsukarimashita
...the car	自動車／カー
	jidō-sha/kā...
...the lorry	トラック
	torakku...
...the motor bike	オートバイ
	ōtobai...
...the bicycle	自転車
	jiten-sha...
...the pedestrian	歩行者
	hokō-sha...
Can you repair the...?	を修理して頂けますか
	...o shūri shite itadakemasu ka

The . . . isn't/aren't working	が故障しています . . . ga koshō shite imasu
. . . brakes	ブレーキ burēki . . .
. . . door	ドア doa . . .
. . . exhaust	排気装置 haiki sōchi . . .
. . . headlights	ヘッドライト heddo raito . . .
. . . radiator	ラジエーター rajiētā . . .
My car is a Nissan/ Toyota/Honda	私の車はニッサン／トヨタ／ ホンダです watashi no kuruma wa Nissan/Toyota/Honda desu
My car has broken down	車がこわれました kuruma ga kowaremashita
Where is the nearest service station for Nissan?	最寄りのニッサンのサービス ・ステーションはどこですか moyori no Nissan no sābisu stēshon wa doko desu ka
traffic accident	交通事故 kōtsū jiko
Look out!	気を付けよ ki o tsukeyo
Help!	助けて tasukete
Please call the police	お巡りさんを呼んでください o-mawari-san o yonde kudasai
I'll call an ambulance	私は救急車を呼びます watashi wa kyūkyū-sha o yobimasu

You may hear:

車の登録番号は何番ですか **kuruma no tōroku bangō wa nan-ban desu ka**	What is your registration number?
ナンバープレートが...番の車 **nanbā purēto ga...ban no kuruma**	Car with registration number...
あなたの...はどこですか **anata no...wa doko desu ka**	Where is your...?
運転免許証 **...unten menkyo shō...**	...driving license
車検証明 **...shaken shōmei...**	...registration certificate
車の保険証 **...kuruma no hoken-sho...**	...certificate of insurance
自動車事故災害保険証 **...jidōsha jiko saigai hoken-shō**	...Green card
パスポート **...pasupōto...**	...passport
何か身分証明になるような物をお持ちですか **nani ka mibun shōmei ni naru yō na mono o o-mochi desu ka**	Have you some identification?
信号は赤でしたか **shingō wa aka desita ka**	Were the lights red?

Where can I find a phone booth?	電話ボックスはどこですか *denwa bokkusu wa doko desu ka*
Are you all right?	大丈夫ですか *daijōbu desu ka*

Is somebody going to make a report?	誰が報告しますか *dare ga hōkoku shimasu ka*
I'll give you my name and address	あなたに私の名前と住所を上げますから *anata ni watashi no namae to jūsho o agemasu kara*
Please contact me if you need me	何かあれば連絡して下さい *nani ka areba renraku shite kudasai*
Is there anyone injured?	怪我をされた方はおられますか *kega o sareta kata wa oraremasu ka*
I'll take you to the hospital	私があなたを病院に連れてきます *watashi ga anata o byōin ni tsurete ikimasu*

You may hear:

罰金を払わなければなりません **bakkin o harawanakereba narimasen**	You will have to pay a fine
スピード違反です **supīdo ihan desu**	You have exceeded the speed limit

traffic lights	信号 *shingō*
green/red/amber lights	青／赤／黄色　信号 *ao/aka/kiiro shingō*
a fine	罰金 *bakkin*
passengers	乗客 *jōkyaku*
I was careless	私は不注意でした *watashi wa fuchūi deshita*
Be careful	気をつけて *ki o tsukete*

Travel by underground

In each station you will find a 'fare adjustment office'. These serve not only as places where you pay excess fares if necessary, but also where you can claim a refund if you paid too much. You can also claim a refund if your train runs late!

Excuse me, where is . . .?	すみません、...はどこですか *sumimasen, . . .wa doko* *desu ka*
. . the underground station	地下鉄の駅 *. . .chika-tetsu no eki. . .*
. . the ticket machine	切符販売機 *. . .kippu hanbai-ki. . .*
. . the map of the under- ground	地下鉄の地図 *. . .chika-tetsu no chizu. . .*
. . the fare adjustment office	運賃精算所 *. . .unchin seisan-jo. . .*
. . the ticket gate	改札口 *. . .kaisatsu-guchi. . .*
Where can I get . . .?	どこで...が買えますか *doko de. . .ga kaemasu ka*
. . a ticket	切符 *. . .kippu. . .*
. . a book of tickets	回数券 *. . .kaisū-ken. . .*
I want to go to . . .	へ行きたいんですが *. . .e ikitai n desu ga*
How much is it?	いくらですか *ikura desu ka*
How often do trains leave from this platform?	このホームから何分置きに電 車が出ますか *kono hōmu kara nan-pun* *oki ni densha ga demasu ka*

Travel

Do I have to change trains?	乗り換えなければなりませ か
	norikae nakereba narimase ka
Which line should I take?	何線に乗ればいいですか
	nani-sen ni noreba ii desu k
How long will it take to get there?	どの位でそこに着きますか
	dono kurai de soko ni tsukimasu ka

Travel by JR train

- The Japanese are very proud of their railway syste and, as it offers probably the most comfortable an efficient rail service in the world, they have every right to be! JR (also known as *Kokutetsu* 国鉄) trains are fast and punctual: with a Japanese rail pass, available only to the visitor, they are economical too.

- When travelling by JR train you cannot do withou a copy of their timetable (called a *jikokuhyo* 時刻表)

- Green cars are the equivalent of first-class carriage You should buy tickets for them at special 'green windows' as there is a surcharge on the standard fare. You should also buy tickets for the bullet tra (*shinkansen*), reserved tickets and 'special' tickets a the green windows.

- The bullet train (*shinkansen* 新幹線) is JR's pride and joy. It runs practically the whole length of Honshu, Japan's largest island, along the Pacific seaboard. Running at frequent intervals (85 trains day), it whisks passengers from Tokyo to Kyoto, a distance of 340 miles, in just three hours of near silent comfort.

88

Types of shinkansen

Tōhoku Shinkansen
  Yamabiko   Limited express
  Aoba   Express
Tōkaidō and San'yō Shinkansen
  Hikari   Limited express
  Kodama   Express
Jōetsu Shinkansen
  Asahi   Limited express
  Toki   Express

- Telephones are available on the *shinkansen* and you can call most major Japanese cities. There are toilets and washbasins in the odd numbered carriages.

- Smoking is not permitted on the majority of trains, but on long-distance trains there are both smoking and non-smoking carriages. Two pieces of luggage per person may be taken into the car free of charge. Porters (*akabō*) are rare and quite expensive, so travel light.

Is there a discount ticket...?	割引切符はありますか ...*waribiki kippu wa arimasu ka*
...for children	子供用の *kodomo yō no...*
...for students	学生用の *gakusei yō no...*
A ticket for...please	行きの切符を一枚下さい ...*iki no kippu o ichi-mai kudasai*
a single (one-way)	片道 *katamichi*
a return (round trip)	往復 *ōfuku*
first-class carriage	一等車 *ittō-sha*

Travel

second-class carriage	二等車 *nitō-sha*
green car	グリーン車 *gurin-sha*
sleeping car	寝台車 *shindai-sha*

You may see:

新幹線（ひかり、こだま） **shinkansen**	bullet train
特急 **tokkyū**	limited express train
急行 **kyūkō**	express train
快速／普通 **kaisoku／futsū**	rapid/local train

I would like...to Tokyo	東京までの...をお願いしま *Tokyō made no...o o-negai* *shimasu*
...a railway/passenger ticket...	乗車券 *...jōsha-ken...*
...a limited express ticket with unreserved seat...	自由席特急券 *...jiyū-seki tokkyū-ken...*
...a limited express ticket with reserved seat...	指定席特急券 *...shitei-seki tokkyū-ken...*
...an express ticket with reserved seat...	急行券 *...kyūko-ken...*

How much is it?	いくらですか *ikura desu ka*
What time does the train leave?	その列車は何時に発車します か *sono ressha wa nan-ji ni hassha shimasu ka*
Do I have to change?	乗り換えなければなりません か *norikae nakereba narimasen ka*
How long does it take?	どの位かかりますか *dono kurai kakarimasu ka*
Is this the right train for...?	この列車は...行きですか *kono ressha wa...iki desu ka*
Is this seat free?	この席はあいていますか *kono seki wa aite imasu ka*
Which platform does the train for Kyoto leave from?	京都行きの列車はどのホーム から発車しますか *Kyōto iki no ressha wa dono hōmu kara hassha shimasu ka*
At what time does the train for...leave?	行きの列車は何時に発車し ますか *...iki no ressha wa nan-ji ni hassha shimasu ka*
Does this train stop in Kobe?	この列車は神戸に止まります か *kono ressha wa Kōbe ni tomarimasu ka*
Which train goes to Nara?	奈良行きの列車はどれですか *Nara iki no ressha wa dore desu ka*
Is this a direct train?	この列車は直通ですか *kono ressha wa chokutsū desu ka*

Is there a dining car in this train?

この列車には食堂車があり
すか
*kono ressha niwa shokudō-
sha ga arimasu ka*

You may hear:

片道ですか往復ですか *katamichi desu ka ōfuku desu ka*	Single or return (one-way or round trip)?
一等ですか二等ですか *ittō desu ka nitō desu ka*	First class or second class?
8番線から／8番ホームか ら *hachi-ban sen kara/hachi- ban hōmu kara*	From platform 8
10分毎（置き）に *jup-pun goto (oki) ni*	Every 10 minutes
切符を拝見させて頂きま すか *kippu o haiken sasete itadakimasu ka*	Could I see your ticket please?

'Station lunches' can be bought either from a kiosk in the station or from a vendor who comes onto the train while it is in the station. They consist of bamboo boxes containing local delicacies (usually cold).

xcuse me, where are...?	すみません、...はどこで すか *sumimasen,...wa doko desu ka*
..the green windows	みどりの窓口 *...midori no madoguchi...*
..the travel bureau	交通公社／旅行案内所 *...kōtsū kōsha/ryokō annai-jo...*
..the ticket office	切符売場 *...kippu uriba...*
..the toilet	トイレ／手洗い／便所 *...toire/tearai/benjo...*
..the left luggage office	手荷物一時預かり所 *...tenimotsu ichiji azukari-jo...*
..the coin lockers	コインロッカー *...koin rokkā...*
..the lost property office	遺失物取扱所 *...ishitsu-butsu toriatsukai-jo...*
..the station kiosk	駅の売店 *...eki no baiten...*
here can I buy lunch in the ation?	どこで駅弁が買えますか *doko de ekiben ga kaemasu ka*

You may hear:

金沢発の列車がまもなく10
番線に到着致します
***Kanazawa hatsu no ressha
ga mamonaku jū-bansen
ni tōchaku itashimasu***

The train from Kanazawa
will shortly arrive at
platform 10

静岡行きの列車は5時2分に
8番線を発車致します
***Shizuoka iki no ressha wa
go-ji ni-fun ni hachi-bansen
o hassha itashimasu***

The train for Shizuoka will
leave at 5.02 from
platform 8

宝塚方面へお越しの方は西
宮北口にてお乗換え下さい
***Takarazuka homen e
okoshi no kata wa
Nishinomiya Kitaguchi nite
o-norikae kudasai***

Passengers for Takarazuka
change trains at
Nishinomiya Kitaguchi

Travel by air

Which flight must I get to go to Hokkaido?	北海道に行くにはどの飛行機に乗ればいいですか *Hokkaidō ni iku niwa dono hikōki ni noreba ii desu ka*
What time is the next flight to London?	次のロンドン行きのフライトは何時ですか *tsugi no London iki no furaito wa nan-ji desu ka*
Do I have to change planes?	飛行機を乗り換えなければなりませんか *hikōki o norikae nakereba narimasen ka*
Where do I have to change planes?	どこで飛行機を乗り換えなければなりませんか *doko de hikōki o norikae nakereba narimasen ka*
From which air terminal does the plane take off?	その飛行機はどの空港ターミナルから出発しますか *sono hikōki wa dono kūkō tāminaru kara shuppatsu shimasu ka*
From which airport does the plane for Canada take off?	カナダ行きの飛行機はどの空港から出発しますか *Kanada iki no hikōki wa dono kūkō kara shuppatsu shimasu ka*
Where is the departure lounge?	出発ロビーはどこですか *shuppatsu robī wa doko desu ka*
Where is the duty-free shop?	免税店はどこですか *menzei-ten wa doko desu ka*
Is the flight delayed?	そのフライトは遅れていますか *sono furaito wa okurete imasu ka*

When do I have to check in?	いつチェックインしなけれ なりませんか *itsu chekku-in shinakereba narimasen ka*
Is there a bus to the airport/town centre?	空港行き／町の中心行きの スはありますか *kūkō iki/machi no chūshin iki no basu wa arimasu ka*
I'd like a seat by the window/in the aisle/at the back	窓際の／内側通路の／後ろ 席をお願いします *mado-giwa no/uchigawa tsūro no/ushiro no seki o o-negai shimasu*
I'd like a seat in a non- smoking area	禁煙席をお願いします *kin'en seki o o-negai shima*

SHOPPING

Shopping in Japan is generally done in three ways.
Firstly, wherever you are in the towns or cities,
there will be small clusters of local shops that are
really more like stalls catering for immediate family
needs. These include butcher's, fishmonger's, fruit
and vegetable shops, grocer's etc.

There are also the 'shopping streets', usually
covered over as protection against rain. They
contain all the above types of shops plus many
others such as book shops, toy shops, clothes and
shoe shops, restaurants, coffee shops and probably
the local post office.

Finally, there are the large department stores,
usually found in the city centre, where it is possible
to buy almost anything. The displays in the
basements of these stores offer an astonishing

variety of foodstuffs from Japan and other
countries. Just browsing can be great fun.

- Most department stores are open six days a week
  (always Saturday and Sunday) and most National
  holidays. Local shops have their own closing days,
  and they always vary. Shopping hours are between
  9 am and 7 pm, and they don't usually close for
  lunch.
- Japanese shopkeepers are scrupulously honest with
  their customers and will count out your change to
  you in meticulous fashion. It's probably true to say
  that you will never be short-changed.
- Bartering is generally unacceptable except in some
  of the high-turnover electrical goods stores in
  Tokyo and Osaka.

I'm looking for...	を捜しています *...o sagashite imasu*
I'm just looking	見ているだけです *mite iru dake desu*
Can you show me...?	を見せてください *...o misete kudasai*
Where's the...department?	売場はどこですか *...uriba wa doko desu ka*
Where do I pay?	支払い場所はどこですか *shiharai basho wa doko desu ka*
Please write it down	それにご記入ください *sore ni go-kinyū kudasai*
I don't want to spend more than...yen	円以上使いたくありません *...en ijō tsukaitaku arimasen*
Can I order it?	それを注文できますか *sore o chūmon dekimasu ka*
Do you accept credit cards?	クレジットカードは使えますか *kurejitto kādo wa tsukaemasu ka*

Shopping

Can I pay by traveller's cheque?	トラベラーズチェックで支払ってもいいですか
	toraberāzuchekku de shiharatte mo ii desu ka

Where is the...?	は、どこですか
	...wa, doko desu ka

...baker's	パン屋
	panya...
...bookshop/stationer's	本屋／文房具屋
	honya/bunbōguya
...butcher's/fish shop	肉屋／魚屋
	nikuya/sakanaya...
...coffee shop	喫茶店
	kissaten...
...tobacconist's	タバコ屋
	tabakoya...
...chemist's	薬（くすり）屋
	kusuriya...
...fruit shop	果物屋
	kudamonoya...
...greengrocer's	八百屋
	yaoya...
...kiosk	売店
	baiten...
...post office	郵便局
	yūbinkyoku...
...shopping centre	商店街
	shōtengai...
...supermarket	スーパー
	sūpā...
...wine store	酒屋
	sakaya...
...market	市場
	ichiba...

Shopping

Have you . . . , please?	は、ありますか . . . wa, arimasu ka
How much is it?	いくらですか ikura desu ka
It's too expensive	高すぎます takasugimasu
Haven't you anything cheaper?	もっと安いのは、ありません か motto yasui no wa, arimasen ka
I'll take it	それに、します sore ni, shimasu
I'll have this one	これを、下さい kore o, kudasai
I prefer that one	その方が、好きです sono hō ga, suki desu
Will you gift-wrap it, please?	それを、贈物用に包んで下さ い sore o, okurimono yō ni tsutsunde kudasai
Are you open every day?	毎日、開いていますか mainichi, aite imasu ka
That's all, thank you	それで結構です sore de kekkō desu
How much do I owe you?	いくらですか ikura desu ka
Here's a 10,000 yen note	はい、1万円札です hai, ichi-man en satsu desu
Excuse me, it's not right	すみません、間違っていま が sumimasen, machigatte imasu ga

I gave you...	私は、あなたに ...を渡しました *watashi wa anata ni... o watashimashita*
You have to give me 300 yen change	あなたからおつり300円を頂かなければなりません *anata kara otsuri sanbyaku-en o itadakanakereba narimasen*
But you gave me only 200 yen back	が、私は200円しか頂きませんでした *ga, watashi wa nihyaku-en shika itadakimasen deshita*

You may hear:

いらっしゃいませ *irasshaimase*	Can I help you?
はい　どうぞ　何か他に *hai dōzo. Nanika hoka ni*	There you are. Anything else?
これで　よろしいですか。 *kore de yoroshii desu ka*	Is that all?
合計六千円です。 *gokei rokusen-en desu*	That's 6000 yen in all
それから四千円のおつりです。 *sore kara yonsen-en no otsuri desu*	And there's 4000 yen change
これを贈物用に包装致しましょうか。 *kore o okurimono yō ni hōsō itashimashō ka*	Shall I gift-wrap it?

General complaints

I want to complain about this	この件で苦情があるのですが *kono ken de kujō ga aru no desu ga*

Shopping

It's too . . .	すぎます . . . *sugimasu*
. . . dark	暗すぎます *kura-sugimasu . . .*
. . . expensive	値段が高すぎます *nedan ga taka-sugimasu . . .*
. . . light (in colour)	薄すぎます *usu-sugimasu . . .*
. . . light (in weight)	軽すぎます *karu-sugimasu . . .*
. . . narrow	狭すぎます *sema-sugimasu . . .*
. . . wide	広すぎます *hiro-sugimasu . . .*
This is shop-soiled	これは店晒しなっています *kore wa tanazarashi ni natte imasu*
This is broken	これは壊れています *kore wa kowarete imasu*
Can you exchange this?	これを交換して頂けますか *kore o kōkan shite itadakemasu ka*
I'd like a refund	払い戻しをお願いします *haraimodoshi o o-negai shimasu*
Here's the receipt	これが領収書です *kore ga ryōshūsho desu*
I bought it yesterday	昨日、それを買いました *kinō sore o kaimashita*
It was a present	それはプレゼントでした *sore wa purezento deshita*

At the department store

Excuse me, where's the department for...?	すみません、...の売場は どこですか *sumimasen,...no uriba wa doko desu ko*
Which floor is it on?	それは何階にありますか *sore wa nan kai ni arimasu ka*

You may hear:	
それは一階にあります *sore wa ik-kai ni arimasu*	It's on the ground floor
それは二階にあります *sore wa ni-kai ni arimasu*	It's on the first floor
三階／四階 *san-kai/yon-kai*	second/third floor
五階／六階 *go-kai/rok-kai*	fourth/fifth floor
地階／屋上 *chikai/okujō*	basement/rooftop

Is there a...?	は、ありますか *...wa, arimasu ka*
Where is the...?	は、どこですか *...wa, doko desu ka*

...escalator	エスカレーター *esukarētā...*
...lift (elevator)	エレベーター *erebētā...*
...cash desk	レジ　お勘定場 *reji/o-kanjō-ba...*
...staircase	階段 *kaidan...*
...exit	出口 *deguchi...*

103

Buying clothes

Have you...?	は、ありますか *...wa, arimasu ka*
...a bathrobe (traditional)	浴衣 *yukata...*
...a blouse	ブラウス *burausu...*
...a bra	ブラジャー *burajā...*
...a cap/hat	帽子 *bōshi...*
...a dress	ドレス *doresu...*
...a handbag	ハンドバック *handobakku...*
...some jeans	ジーパン *jīpan...*
...some panties	パンティー *pantī...*
...a raincoat	レインコート *reinkōto...*
...some pyjamas	パジャマ *pajama...*
...some shirts (for men)	ワイシャツ *waishatsu...*
...some shoes	靴　シューズ *kutsu/shūzu...*
...some socks	靴下 *kutsushita...*
...a suit (for men)	背広 *sebiro...*
...a sweater	セーター *sētā...*

Shopping

. . some swimming trunks	海水パンツ *kaisui pantsu.* . .
. . a T-shirt	Ｔ－シャツ *ti-shatsu.* . .
. . some tights	タイツ *taitsu.* . .
. . some trousers	ズボン *zubon.* . .
. . some underpants	パンツ *pantsu.* . .

What size are you?	あなたのサイズは *anata no saizu wa*
I take size 11	11です *ju-ichi desu*

See page 135 for clothes sizes.

What's this coat made of?	このコートの生地は何ですか か *kono kōto no kiji wa nan desu ka*

It's made of. . .	（その生地は）. . .です *(sono kiji wa).* . . *desu*

. . cotton	木綿 *momen.* . .
. . linen	リンネル *rinneru.* . .
. . silk	絹 *kinu.* . .
. . wool	羊毛 *yōmō*
. . leather	革 *kawa.* . .
. . nylon	ナイロン *nairon.* . .

You may hear:

どんな物がご入用でしょうか *donna mono ga go-nyūyō deshō ka*	What sort of thing are you looking for?
どんな色がよろしいですか *donna iro ga yoroshii desu ka*	What colour do you prefer?
失礼ですが、お客様のサイズは *shitsurei desu ga o-kyaku-sama no saizu wa*	Excuse me, what size are you?
綿と純毛ではどちらがいいですか *men to junmō dewa dochira ga ii desu ka*	Do you want it in cotton or pure wool?
何か他にございませんか *nani ka hoka ni gozaimasen ka.*	Would you like anything else?

Buying food and drink

At the supermarket

a litre of milk	牛乳／ミルク1リットル *gyūnyū/miruku ichi-rittoru*
a packet of butter	バター1箱 *batā hito-hako*
a packet of ham	ハム1袋 *hamu hito-fukuro*
a box of eggs	たまご1箱 *tamago hito-hako*
a jar of strawberry jam	苺ジャム1瓶 *ichigo jamu hito-bin*
a bottle of sauce	ソース1瓶／1本 *sōsu hito-bin/ip-pon*

packet of biscuits	ビスケット1袋
	bisuketto hito-fukuro
kilo of potatoes	じゃがいも1キロ（グラム）
	jagaimo ichi-kiro (guramu)
00 grams of beef	牛肉300グラム
	gyūniku sanbyaku-guramu
ve tomatoes	トマト5個
	tomato go-ko

At the baker's

You should not miss the opportunity to try bean jam. It is the result of boiling beans with sugar, and is combined with pastry etc to form a variety of cakes and buns. It is a very popular type of confectionery and is traditionally served with green tea.

loaf of bread	食パン
	shoku-pan
ick sliced (for toast)	厚切り（トースト用）
	atsugiri (tōsuto-yō)
in sliced (for sandwiches)	薄切り（サンドイッチ用）
	usugiri (sandoitch-yō)
chocolate gateau	チョコレートケーキ
	chokorēto kēki
strawberry cake	ストロベリーケーキ
	sutoroberī kēki
pissants	クロワッサン
	kurowassan
ughnuts	ドーナツ
	dōnatsu
eam puffs	シュークリーム
	shūkurīmu
bean-jam bun	あんパン
	an pan
cream bun	クリームパン
	kurīmu pan

At the fruitshop

some of that fruit	その果物数個 *sono kudamono sūko*
six of the satsumas	そのみかん6個 *sono mikan rok-ko*
three apples	りんご3個 *ringo san-ko*
a kilo of bananas	バナナ1キロ *banana ichi-kiro*
a bunch of grapes	葡萄1房 *budō hito-fusa*
some of the oranges at 500 yen	1山500円のオレンジ *hito-yama gohyaku-en no orenji*
two kilos of peaches	桃2キロ *momo ni-kiro*
a box of melons	メロン1箱 *meron hito-hako*
400 grams of cherries	さくらんぼ400グラム *sakuranbo yonhyaku-guramu*
Can you wrap this fruit for a present?	この果物を贈物用に包んで ただけますか *kono kudamono o okurimono yō ni tsutsund itadakemasu ka*
Two large pears please	大きい梨を2つ下さい *ōkii nashi o futatsu kudas*

At the butcher's

meat	肉 *niku*
beef/pork	牛肉／豚肉 *gyūniku/butaniku*
chicken	鳥肉 *toriniku/keiniku*

108

Can I have 300 grams f...?	（を）300グラム下さい ...(o) sanbyaku-guramu kudasai
..beef steak	ステーキ用牛肉 sutēki yō gyūniku...
..beef for curry or stew	カレー・シチュー用牛肉 karē・shichū yō gyūniku...
..beef for sukiyaki	すきやき用牛肉 sukiyaki yō gyūniku...
..beef for shabu-shabu	しゃぶしゃぶ用牛肉 shabu-shabu yō gyuniku...
..minced beef	牛ミンチ gyū minchi...
..beef liver	牛レバー gyū rebā...
..roasted beef	ローストビーフ rōsuto bifu...
..bacon	ベーコン bēkon...
..sausages	ソーセージ sōsēji...
..ham	ハム hamu...
..pork fillet	豚ヒレ肉 buta hireniku...
eg (chicken)	骨付もも肉 honetsuki momoniku
reast (chicken)	むね肉 muneniku

At the fishmonger's

sh	魚 sakana

Shopping

cod	鱈 *tara*
crab	カニ *kani*
eel	鰻 *unagi*
shrimp/prawn/lobster	海老 *ebi*
mackerel	鯖 *saba*
octopus	蛸 *tako*
salmon	鮭 *sake*
sardine	鰯 *iwashi*
plaice/sole	鰈 *karei-hirame*
sea bream	鯛 *tai*
squid/cuttlefish	烏賊 *ika*
tuna	鮪 *maguro*

Drinks

I'd like a bottle of...	1本下さい *...ip-pon kudasai*
I'd like a glass of...	1杯下さい *...ip-pai kudasai*
I'd like a can of...	一缶下さい *...hito-kan kudasai*
...sake	酒 *sake...*

. . beer	ビール *biru . . .*
. . whisky	ウイスキー *uisukī . . .*
. . red wine	赤ワイン *aka wain . . .*
. . white wine	白ワイン *shiro wain . . .*
. . gin and tonic	ジントニック *jin tonikku . . .*
. . brandy	ブランデー *burandē . . .*
. . whisky with water	水割り *mizuwari . . .*
. . single/double whisky	シングル／ダブル　ウイスキー *singuru/daburu uisukī*
. . on the rocks	オンザロックで *onzarokku de*

Souvenirs

You may see:

風鈴／提灯 **fūrin/chōchin**	wind-bells/lantern
扇子／団扇 **sensu/uchiwa**	folding fan/fan
達磨 **daruma**	buddha doll
傘 **kasa**	umbrella (traditional)
人形／刀 **ningyō/katana**	doll (traditional)/sword
着物 **kimono**	kimono

浴衣 *yukata*	Japanese dressing gown
陶器・焼き物 *tōki · yakimono*	ceramics/pottery
漆器 *shikki*	lacquerware
おもちゃ／真珠 *omocha/shinju*	toys/pearls
時計 *tokei*	watch

Photography

I'd like...	がほしいのですが *...ga hoshii no desu ga*
...a black and white film	白黒フイルム *shiro-kuro fuirumu...*
...a colour film	カラーフイルム *karā fuirumu...*
...a film for slides	スライド用フイルム *suraido yō fuirumu...*
...a film of 12/24/36 explosures	12／24／36枚撮りフイル *jū-ni/nijū-yon/sanjū-roku-mai dori fuirumu...*
...a film for this camera	このカメラ（用）のフイル *kono kamera (yō) no fuirumu...*
How much do you charge for developing?	現像代はいくらですか *genzō-dai wa ikura desu ka*
When will the photos be ready?	写真はいつ出来上がります *shashin wa itsu dekiagarimasu ka*

SERVICES

Japan is extremely well served with banks, and almost all of them will change your currency or traveller's cheques into yen (¥ or 円) upon presentation of your passport. Banks are open on weekdays from 9am to 3pm but are closed at weekends and national holidays.

Local post offices are open Monday to Friday from 9am to 5pm, and larger branches open on Saturdays until midday. You can buy stamps at tobacco shops as well as post offices.

The recovery rate for lost property, even jewellery, cameras, wallets and purses, is very high, so you should report your loss to the nearest police station. If you have lost or left something on the train, you should make immediate enquiries at the lost property office (遺失物取扱所 *ishitsu butsu toriatsukai-jo*) at a main station.

At the bank or exchange bureau

Where is the exchange window?	両替口はどこですか *ryōgae-guchi wa doko desu ka*
I would like to change...	を変えたいのですが *...o kaetai no desu ga*
...a traveller's cheque	トラベラーズチェック *toraberāzu chekku...*
...some pounds sterling	英国のポンド *Eikoku no pondo...*
...some US dollars	アメリカのドル *Amerika no doru...*
...some Canadian dollars	カナダのドル *Kanada no doru...*
...some Australian dollars	オーストラリアのドル *Ōsutoraria no doru...*
I would like to cash this cheque	このチェックを現金に変え いのですか *kono chekku o genkin ni kaetai no desu ga*
Please change this into yen	これを円に両替して下さい *kore o en ni ryōgae shite kudasai*
What is today's exchange rate?	今日の為替レートはいくら すか *kyō no kawase rēto wa ikur desu ka*
What is your rate of commission?	手数料／コミッションはい らですか *tesūryō/komisshon wa ikur desu ka...*
Is it free?	無料ですか *muryō desu ka*

Services

Is it included?	入っていますか *haitte imasu ka*
Here is my passport	はい、パスポートです *hai, pasupōto desu*
Here it is	はい、どうぞ *hai, dōzo*
Please give me smaller change	細かくして下さい *komakaku shite kudasai*
Please give it to me in 10,000-yen notes	1万円札でお願いします *ichiman-en-satsu de o-negai shimasu*

You may hear:

パスポートを見せてください **pasupōto o misete kudasai**	Please show me your passport
いくら御入用ですか **ikura go-nyūyō desu ka**	How much do you want?
どのように致しましょうか **dono yō ni itashimashō ka**	How would you like it?
5千円札がよろしいですか **gosen-en satsu ga yoroshii desu ka**	Do you want it in 5000-yen notes?
ここにサインして下さい **koko ni sain shite kudasai**	Sign here, please
これを隣の窓口へお持ち下さい **kore o tonari no madoguchi e o-mochi kudasai**	Please take this to the next window
全部で11万円になります **zenbu de jū-ichiman-en ni narimasu**	That makes 110,000 yen altogether

Monetary values

一万円札 *ichiman-en satsu*	10,000-yen note
五千円札 *gosen-en satsu*	5000-yen note
千円札 *sen-en satsu*	1000-yen note
五百円札／硬貨 *gohyaku-en satsu/kōka*	500-yen note/coin
百円硬貨 *hyaku-en kōka*	100-yen coin
五十円硬貨 *gojū-en kōka*	50-yen coin
十円硬貨 *jū-en kōka*	10-yen coin
五円硬貨 *go-en kōka*	5-yen coin
一円硬貨 *ichi-en kōka*	1-yen coin

account	口座 *kōza*
balance	残高 *zandaka*
deposit/bank account	預金 *yokin*
withdrawal	払い戻し金 *harai modoshikin*
account number	口座番号 *kōza bangō*
notes	紙幣、札 *shihei, satsu*
total	合計 *gōkei*

Services

interest	利子 *rishi*
cheque	小切手 *kogitte*
cash	現金 *genkin*
foreign currency	外貨 *gaika*
foreign exchange	外国為替 *gaikoku kawase*
exchange rate	為替レート *kawase rēto*
deposit statement	預金明細書 *yokin meisai-sho*
receipt	領収書 *ryōshū-sho*
reduction	差し引き *sashihiki*
transfer	繰り入れ *kuriire*
credit card	クレジット・カード *kurejitto kādo*
money value	金額 *kingaku*
PIN number	暗証番号 *anshō bangō*
stamp	印鑑 *inkan*
cheque card	バンクカード *banku kādo*
bankbook	預金通帳 *yokin tsūchō*
payment	支払い *shiharai*

Post Office

I can't find the post office	郵便局が見つからないのです が *yūbin-kyoku ga mitsukaranai no desu ga*
Do you know where . . . is?	はどこかご存じですか *. . . wa doko ka go-zonji desu ka*
. . . the post office	郵便局 *yūbin-kyoku . . .*
. . . letter box (a mailbox)	ポスト *posuto . . .*

I'd like to send . . .	を送りたいのですが、 *. . . o okuritai no desu ga*

. . . a letter	手紙 *tegami . . .*
. . . a post card	はがき *hagaki . . .*
. . . a telegram	電報 *denpō . . .*
. . . a parcel	小包 *kozutsumi . . .*

I'd like to send this . . .	これを . . . 送りたいのですが *kore . . . okuritai no desu ga*

. . . by express	速達で *. . . sokutatsu de . . .*
. . . by registered post	書留で *. . . kakidome de . . .*
. . . by surface mail	船便で *. . . funabin de . . .*
. . . by airmail	航空便で *. . . kōkūbin de . . .*

...to Britain	英国へ
	...Eikoku e...
...to the USA	米国／アメリカへ
	...Beikoku/Amerika e...
How much does it cost to send this parcel to Australia?	この小包をオーストラリアに送るにはいくらかかりますか
	kono kozutsumi o Ōsutoraria ni okuru niwa ikura kakarimasu ka
How long will it take for this letter to get to this address?	この手紙はどのくらいでこの宛先に着きます
	kono tegami wa dono kurai de kono atesaki ni tsukimasu ka

| I would like... | （を）下さい |
| | ...(o) kudasai |

...three post cards	官製はがまを三枚
	kansei hagaki o san-mai...
...two aerogrammes	航空書簡／エアログラムを二枚
	kōkū shokan/earoguramu o ni-mai...
...five 70-yen stamps	七十円切手を五枚
	nanajū-en kitte o go-mai...
...a phonecard	テレフォンカード
	terefon kādo...

| At which window are stamps sold? | 切手はどの窓口で売られていますか |
| | kitte wa dono madoguchi de urarete imasu ka |

You may hear:

それを秤の上にのせてください　Put it on the scales, please

sore o hakari no ue ni nosete kudasai

この用紙に記入してください　Fill in this form, please

kono yōshi ni kinyū shite kudasai

ここにサインしてください　Sign here, please

koko ni sain shite kudasai

船便でですか、航空便でですか　By surface mail or by airmail?

funabin de desu ka kōkūbin de desu ka

全部で9250円です　That's 9250 yen altogether

zenbu de kyūsen-nihyaku-gojū-en desu

中には何が入っていますか　What's inside?

naka niwa nani ga haitte imasu ka

20kg 以上ありますね　That's over 20kg

nijuk-kiro ijō arimasu ne

もう一度梱包し直してください　Can you repack it?

mō ichi-do konpō shinaoshite kudasai

Telephoning

- Public telephones are plentiful, and it is cheap to make local calls. (Use the red, blue and pink phones for local calls). The procedure is simple: lift the receiver and put a ¥10 coin into the slot (¥10 buys about a two- to three-minute local call). Dial when you hear the dialling tone. You will be connected directly. After your call, all unused coins will be returned.

For long distance calls, use the yellow phones that take ¥100 coins and when dialling directly abroad, you'll have to find one of the green ISD (International Subscriber Dialling) phones. Where these phones are unavailable, go through KDD (Kokusai Denshin Denwa) Ltd who employ multi-lingual operators. You'll have to give the operator all the information for placing your call, including your own number, and wait for the return call and the connection you require. Calls via the operator can be made by dialling 0051.

Hello	もしもし *moshi moshi*
Is that Mr Yamada's house?	そちらは山田さんのお宅ですか *sochira wa Yamada-san no o-taku desu ka*
May I speak to your husband?	ご主人（様）をお願いします *go-shujin-(sama) o o-negai shimasu*
I'm sorry	失礼しました *shitsurei shimashita*
I'm ringing 445-3876	445-3876に電話を掛けています *yon-yon-go no san-hachi-nana-roku ni denwa o kakete imasu*
I'll ring you later	後程、お電話します *nochihodo, o-denwa shimasu*

Business calls

Hello, this is Mr Smith from JCCL calling	もしもし、JCCL のスミスと申します *moshimoshi, jei-shi-shi-eru no Sumisu to mōshimasu*

You may hear:

はい、そうですが *hai, sō desu ga*	Yes, that's right.
どんなご用件でしょうか *donna go-yōken deshō ka*	What can I do for you?
どちらさまですか *dochira-sama desu ka*	Who's calling, please?
少々お待ちください *shōshō o-machi kudasai*	Hold the line, please
今、留守ですが *ima rusu desu ga*	He's not at home now
今、外出中ですが *ima gaishutsu-chū desu ga*	He's out at the moment
何か伝えることがありますか *nanika tsutaeru koto ga arimasu ka*	Would you like to leave a message?
いいえ、ちがいます *iie, chigaimasu*	No, you've got the wrong number
どの番号にお掛けですか *dono bangō ni o-kake desu ka*	What number are you calling?

Can I speak to Mr Suzuki in the personnel section?	人事課の鈴木さんお願いします *jinji-ka no Suzuki-san o-negai shimasu*
I want extension 357, please	内線357番をお願いします *naisen sanbyaku-gojū-nana-ban o o-negai shimasu*
Can you transfer this call to extension 426?	この電話を内線426番に回して下さい *kono denwa o naisen yonhyaku-nijū-roku-ban ni mawashite kudasai*

You may hear:

申し訳ありませんが
moshiwake arimasen ga

I'm sorry, but...

佐藤は席を外しております
Satō wa seki o hazushite orimasu

Mr Sato has stepped out for a moment

山下は出張中です
Yamashita wa shutchō-chū desu

Mr Yamashita is away on business

鈴木は只今、会議中です
Suzuki wa tadaima kaigi-chū desu

Mr Suzuki is in a meeting at the moment

Lost property

Where is the nearest police box?

最寄りの交番はどこですか
moyori no kōban wa doko desu ka

Is there a lost-property office at this station?

この駅には遺失物取扱所はありますか
kono eki niwa ishitsu butsu toriatsukaijo wa arimasu ka

I've lost...

を失くしました
...o nakushimashita

..my wallet

財布／札入れ
saifu/satsuire...

..my handbag

ハンドバック
hando bakku...

..my suitcase

スーツケース
sūtsukēsu...

..my ring/umbrella

指輪／傘
yubiwa/kasa...

..my passport

パスポート
pasupōto...

I think I lost it . . .	失くしたと思います . . . *nakushita to omoimasu*
. . . on the train	汽車／列車の中で *kisha/ressha no naka de . .*
. . . on the bus	バスの中で *basu no naka de . . .*
. . . at the underground station	地下鉄の駅で *chikatetsu no eki de . . .*
. . . on the Hankyu train	阪急電車の中で *Hankyū densha no naka de . . .*
. . . on the street	道路上で *dōro jō de . . .*
I noticed I'd lost my purse . . .	財布を失くしたことに気が付きました . . . *saifu o nakushita koto ni ki ga tsukimashita*
. . . today	今日 *kyō . . .*
. . . this morning	今朝 *kesa . . .*
. . . yesterday	昨日 *kinō . . .*
. . . last night	昨夜 *sakuya . . .*
My name is on it	落し物には名前が書いてあります *otoshimono niwa namae ga kaite arimasu*

The colour is brown	色は茶色です *iro wa chairo desu*
The shape is square	形は 真四角／正方形 です *katachi wa ma-shikaku/* *seihō-kei desu*
The size is small/medium/ large	サイズは 小さい／中位／大 きい です *saizu wa chiisai/chūkurai* *ōkii desu*
It's . . . m long	長さは...メートルです *nagasa wa . . . mētoru desu*
It's . . . cm wide	幅は...センチです *haba wa . . . senchi desu*
It's . . . cm thick	厚みは...センチです *atsumi wa . . . senchi desu*
It's . . . mm across	直径は...ミリです *chokkei wa . . . miri desu*
It's made of. . .	ででできています *. . . de dekite imasu*
. . . gold/silver/platinum	金／銀／プラチナ *kin/gin/purachina . . .*
. . . metal	金属 *kinzoku. . .*
. . . leather	革 *kawa. . .*
. . . plastic	プラスティック *purasutikku. . .*
. . . nylon	ナイロン *nairon. . .*

You may hear:

どんなご用件でしょうか ***donna go-yōken deshō ka***	What can I do for you?
何を失くしましたか ***nani o nakushimashita ka***	What did you lose?
どんな鞄ですか ***donna kaban desu ka***	What's the bag like?
いつ失くしましたか ***itsu nakushimashita ka***	When did you lose it?
どこでなくしましたか ***doko de nakushimashita ka***	Where did you lose it?
中には何が入っていましたか ***naka niwa nani ga haitte imashita ka***	What was there inside?
それについて詳しく説明して下さい ***sore ni tsuite kuwashiku setsumei shite kudasai***	Can you give me some details, please?
連絡先を言って下さい ***renrakusaki o itte kudasai***	Tell me where I can contact you
知らせが入り次第連絡します ***shirase ga hairi shidai renraku shimasu***	As soon as I get news, I will contact you

Cleaning and repairs

I'm looking for...	を捜しているのですか ...*o sagashite iru no desu ka*
Do you know where I can find...?	はどこかご存じですか ...*wa dokoka go-zonji desu ka*
...a dry cleaner's	ドライクリーニング屋 *dorai kurīningu-ya...*

Services

. . a garage	ガレージ／車庫 *garēji/shako . . .*
. . a laundrette	コインランドリー *koin randorī . . .*
. . a shoe/watch repairer	靴／時計　の修理屋 *kutsu/tokei no shūri-ya . . .*
My watch isn't working	時計が壊れました *tokei ga kowaremashita*
My car has broken down	車が故障してしまいました *kuruma ga koshō shite shimaimashita*
How much is it to dry clean a suit?	スーツのクリーニング代はいくらですか *sūtsu no kurīningu-dai wa ikura desu ka*
When will it be ready?	いつ出来上がりますか *itsu dekiagarimasu ka*
How long will it take?	どの位かかりますか *dono kurai kakarimasu ka*
Can it be ready earlier?	もっと早くできませんか *motto hayaku dekimasen ka*

Information

Where is the travel bureau?	交通公社／旅行案内所はどこです *kōtsū-kōsha/ryokō annai-jo wa doko desu ka*
I want to know about . . . in this town	この町の . . . について知りたいのですが *kono machi no . . . ni tsuite shiritai no desu ga*
. . hotels/Japanese-style hotels	ホテル／旅館 *. . . hoteru/ryokan . . .*

. . . castles	お城 . . . *o-shiro* . . .
. . . shrines/temples	神社／お寺 . . . *jinja/o-tera* . . .
. . . museums	博物館 . . . *hakubutsu-kan* . . .
. . . cinemas	映画館 . . . *eiga-kan* . . .
. . . exhibitions	展覧会 . . . *tenran-kai* . . .
. . . festivals	お祭り . . . *o-matsuri* . . .
. . . sports facilities	運動施設 . . . *undō-shisetsu* . . .
. . . theatres	劇場 . . . *gekijō* . . .

Have you . . . ?	は、ありますか . . . *wa, arimasu ka*

. . . some pamphlets/ brochures/leaflets	パンフレット *panfuretto* . . .
. . . a list of hotels	ホテルの一覧表 *hoteru no ichiran-hyō* . . .
. . . a map of the town	この町の地図 *kono machi no chizu* . . .

Useful questions

Where is . . . ?	は、どこですか . . . *wa doko desu ka*
When does it begin?	いつ始まりますか *itsu hajimarimasu ka*
When does it end?	いつ終りますか *itsu owarimasu ka*
What's the price of . . . ?	は、いくらですか . . . *wa ikura desu ka*

ESSENTIAL INFORMATION

Numbers

1	一	*ichi*	12	十二	*jū-ni*
2	二	*ni*	13	十三	*jū-san*
3	三	*san*	20	二十	*nijū*
4	四	*shi/yon/yo*	21	二十一	*nijū-ichi*
5	五	*go*	30	三十	*sanjū*
6	六	*roku*	40	四十	*yonjū, shijū*
7	七	*shichi/nana*	50	五十	*gojū*
8	八	*hachi*	60	六十	*rokujū*
9	九	*kyū/ku*	70	七十	*shichijū, nanajū*
10	十	*jū*	80	八十	*hachijū*
11	十一	*jū-ichi*	90	九十	*kyūjū*

100	百	*hyaku*	1000	千	*sen*
200	二百	*nihyaku*	3000	三千	*sanzen*
300	三百	*sanbyaku*	8000	八千	*hassen*
400	四百	*yonhyaku*	10,000	一万	*ichiman*
600	六百	*roppyaku*	100,000	十万	*jūman*
700	七百	*nanahyaku*	1,000,000	百万	*hyakuman*
800	八百	*happyaku*	10,000,000	千万	*senman*
900	九百	*kyūhyaku*	100,000,000	一億	*ichioku*

Ordinal numbers

Ordinal numbers can be created from cardinal numbers by the addition of a suffix *ban* or *ban-me*, or a prefix *dai*.

first	*ichi-ban(me)*	or	*dai-ichi*
second	*ni-ban(me)*	or	*dai-ni*
third	*san-ban(me)*	or	*dai-san*
fourth	*yon-ban(me)*	or	*dai-yon*
fifth	*go-ban(me)*	or	*dai-go*
sixth	*roku-ban(me)*	or	*dai-roku*
seventh	*nana-ban(me)*	or	*dai-nana*
	shichi-ban(me)	or	*dai-shichi*
eighth	*hachi-ban(me)*	or	*dai-hachi*
ninth	*kyū-ban(me)*	or	*dai-kyū*
	ku-ban(me)	or	*dai-ku*
tenth	*jū-ban(me)*	or	*dai-jū*

Counting and counters

- Counting in Japanese can be complicated because different 'counting' words are used for different shaped objects. To complicate matters further, there is a Japanese system from 1 to 10 and another system borrowed from the Chinese that will count to any number.
- The Japanese system for counting objects is:

一つ	hitotsu	*one*	六つ	muttsu	*six*
二つ	futatsu	*two*	七つ	nanatsu	*seven*
三つ	mittsu	*three*	八つ	yattsu	*eight*
四つ	yottsu	*four*	九つ	kokonotsu	*nine*
五つ	itsutsu	*five*	十	tō	*ten*

- Counters are words used with numbers to provide a link between the number and the object being counted. There is no equivalent in English, although the word 'bottles' in the phrase 'two bottles of wine' is close, in that it gives a shape to the wine.

  Here are some common counters for counting objects:

  Mai (枚) is used for counting thin, flat objects, eg stamps, sheets of paper, cards
  ichi-mai, ni-mai etc
  Hyaku-en kitte o ni-mai o-negai shimasu
  Please give me two ¥100 stamps

  Sai (才) is used for counting age.
  is-sai, ni-sai etc
  Kare wa jū-ni-sai desu
  He is 12 years old

  Hon (本) is used for counting 'long' objects.
  ip-pon, ni-hon, san-bon, yon-hon
  Bīru o san-bon kudasai
  Please give me three bottles of beer.

- It's difficult to learn all the different counters in Japanese, though good Japanese requires that you do. However, just to make yourself understood, you can get away with the Japanese counting system for counting objects up to 10.

Days of the week

Sunday	日曜日 *nichiyōbi*	Thursday	木曜日 *mokuyōbi*
Monday	月曜日 *getsuyōbi*	Friday	金曜日 *kin'yōbi*
Tuesday	火曜日 *kayōbi*	Saturday	土曜日 *doyōbi*
Wednesday	水曜日 *suiyōbi*		

the day before yesterday	一昨日 *ototoi*
yesterday	昨日 *kinō*
today	今日 *kyō*
tomorrow	明日 *asu/ashita*
the day after tomorrow	明後日 *asatte*
last year	去年／昨年 *kyonen/sakunen*
this year	今年 *kotoshi*
next year	来年 *rainen*
last Friday	先週の金曜日 *senshū no kin'yōbi*

Months

January	一月 *ichigatsu*		July	七月 *shichigatsu*
February	二月 *nigatsu*		August	八月 *hachigatsu*
March	三月 *sangatsu*		September	九月 *kugatsu*
April	四月 *shigatsu*		October	十月 *jūgatsu*
May	五月 *gogatsu*		November	十一月 *jūichigatsu*
June	六月 *rokugatsu*		December	十二月 *jūnigatsu*

Dates

1st	一日 *tsuitachi*	6th	六日 *muika*	11th	十一日 *jū-ichi-nic*
2nd	二日 *futsuka*	7th	七日 *nanoka*		
3rd	三日 *mikka*	8th	八日 *yōka*		
4th	四日 *yokka*	9th	九日 *kokonoka*		
5th	五日 *itsuka*	10th	十日 *tōka*		

- Add *nichi* to the number of the day after 11th. The 14th, 20th, and 24th are exceptions

14th	十四日 *jū-yokka*	24th	二十四日 *nijū-yokka*
20th	二十日 *hatsuka*		

- The Japanese count out the full number in the western year, e.g. **1991** *sen-kyūhyaku-kyūju-ichi-nen*. When stating the date in Japanese, the year comes first, followed by the month and finally the day.

Time

n the morning (am)	朝／午前 *asa/gozen*
n the afternoon (pm)	昼／午後 *hiru/gogo*
n the evening	夜／晩 *yoru/ban*
oon, midday	正午／昼の12時 *shōgo/hiru no jū-ni-ji*
nidnight	真夜中／夜の12時 *mayonaka/yoru no jū-ni-ji*

Telling the time

o'clock	1時 *ichi-ji*		7 o'clock	7時 *shichi-ji*	
o'clock	2時 *ni-ji*		8 o'clock	8時 *hachi-ji*	
o'clock	3時 *san-ji*		9 o'clock	9時 *ku-ji*	
o'clock	4時 *yo-ji*		10 o'clock	10時 *jū-ji*	
o'clock	5時 *go-ji*		11 o'clock	11時 *jū-ichi-ji*	
o'clock	6時 *roku-ji*		12 o'clock	12時 *jū-ni-ji*	

ast (often omitted)	過ぎ *sugi*
o (between the half hour nd the hour)	前 *mae*
our	時 *ji*
inute	分 *fun*
econd	秒 *byō*

- Japanese has no equivalent for the English word 'quarter' when expressing the time. The quarter is always expressed in Japanese as *jū-go-fun* (15 minutes).
- When telling the time, the largest unit comes first, e.g.

1986年8月18日午前九時半

Sen-kyūhyaku-hachijū-roku-nen, Hachigatsu, Jū-hachi-nichi, gozen ku-ji han

half past nine am, 18th August 1986

jup-pun (*jū*)	= =	10 minutes for 11–19 minutes, plus...	*ip-pun*		= 1 minute
			ni-fun		= 2 minutes
nijup-pun (*nijū*)	=	20 minutes for 21–29 minutes, plus...	*san-pun*		= 3 minutes
sanjup-pun (*sanjū*)	=	30 minutes for 31–39 minutes, plus...	*yon-fun* *yon-pun*		= 4 minutes
			go-fun		= 5 minutes
yonjup-pun (*yonjū*)	=	40 minutes for 41–49 minutes, plus...	*rop-pun*		= 6 minutes
gojup-pun (*gojū*)	=	50 minutes for 51–59 minutes, plus...	*nana-fun* *schichi-fun*		= 7 minutes
rokujup-pun	=	60 minutes	*hap-pun* *hachi-fun*		= 8 minutes
			kyū-fun		= 9 minutes

What's the time now?	今、何時ですか	*ima nan-ji desu ka*
It's just six o'clock	ちょうど6時です	*chōdo roku-ji desu*
It's half past three	3時半です	*san-ji han desu*
It's ten minutes to five	5時10分前です	*go-ji juppun mae desu*
It's fifteen minutes past four	4時15分（過ぎ）です	*yo-ji jū-go-fun (sugi) desu*

Clothes sizes

Men's suits and overcoats

British	34	36	38	40	42	44	46
American	34	36	38	40	42	44	46
Japanese	S		M		L		LL

Men's shirts

British	14	14½	15	15½	16	16½	17
American	14	14½	15	15½	16	16½	17
Japanese	36	37	38	39	40	41	42

Men's shoes

British	5½	6	7	8	9	10	11
American	5½	6½	7½	8½	9½	10½	11½
Japanese	24½		26		27½	28	29

Women's dresses and suits

British	32	34	36	38	40	42	44
American	10	12	14	16	18	20	22
Japanese	9	11	13	15	17	19	21

Women's shoes

British	4½	5	5½	6	6½	7	7½
American	6	6½	6½	7½	8	8½	9
Japanese	23	23½	23½	24½	25	25½	26

Public holidays in Japan

January 1st
New Year's Day

正月
shōgatsu

January 15th
Adults' Day

成人の日
seijin no hi

February 11th
National Foundation Day

建国記念日
kenkoku kinen bi

March 20th or 21st
Vernal Equinox Day

春分の日
shunbun no hi

April 29th
Green Day

緑の日
midori no hi

May 3rd
Constitution Memorial Day

憲法記念日
kenpō kinen bi

May 5th
Children's Day

子供の日
kodomo no hi

September 15th
Respect for the Aged Day

敬老の日
keirō no hi

September 23rd
Autumn Equinox Day

秋分の日
shūbun no hi

October 10th
Health–Sports Day

体育の日
taiiku no hi

November 3rd
Culture Day

文化の日
bunka no hi

November 23rd
Labour Thanksgiving Day

勤労感謝の日
kinrō kansha no hi

December 23rd
The Emperor's Birthday

天皇誕生日
tennō tanjō bi

The weather

- Japan is over two thousand miles long, stretching like a crescent moon from the colder north to the sub-tropical south. The climate varies quite considerably from region to region, but most of the country enjoys a warm, temperate climate with four distinct seasons.

- The rainy season (梅雨期 *tsuyu*) in June and July is probably the most unpleasant time of the year, with spring and autumn being the best seasons.

- On the Pacific coast, summers are very hot and humid. On the Japan Sea side, the winter winds from Siberia bring very heavy snow falls.

- If you happen to be in Japan during the hot, summer months, it is essential that you wear the lightest clothes possible. Some kind of insect repellent is a must too. Mosquitoes are a real nuisance, and anti-mosquito coils (蚊取り線香 *katori senkō*) need to be used if you are going to get any sleep at night.

- The typhoon (台風 *taifū*) season blows into Japan any time between July and the end of October. These often devastating cyclonic storms require a degree of respect. Warnings are issued on TV and on the radio, but only in Japanese. The Japanese have developed a stoic attitude to typhoons, but the most recent one (1990) claimed at least 40 lives, and untold numbers were left homeless. If you are in Japan when a typhoon alert is sounded:
  - Get inside and stay inside.
  - Check that you have emergency lighting equipment like candles, torches, lamps etc.
  - Close all windows, draw blinds and shutters.

Important words

台風警報	*tai-fū kei-hō*	Typhoon alarm
大雨	*ō-ame*	Very heavy rain
解除	*kai-jo*	The all`clear

- The Japanese archipelago is volcanic and subject to regular earthquakes, but most of them are weak and pass without notice. Occasionally, a big one does occur. The Great Earthquake of 1923 struck Yokohama and Tokyo with such devastation that it is now etched in Japanese history.

- Should you be involved in an earthquake, don't panic and remember the following points:
  - If you are indoors, get under a desk or table, preferably against an inside wall and away from windows.
  - Put out fires and unplug electrical appliances. Do not use matches or lighters.
  - If you are outdoors, move away from buildings as much as possible. Keep away from overhead power cables.
  - Stay in the middle of the street.
  - If you are in a car, come to a stop and stay in the car until the earthquake has ended.

Emergency calls

- Ring 110 for police and 119 for fire and ambulance.

Please send the police	警察、お願いします *keisatsu o-negai shimasu*
Please send an ambulance	救急車、お願いします *kyūkyu-sha o-negai shimasu*
There is a fire	火事です *kaji desu*

Visiting the Japanese at home

In the happy event that you are invited to visit a Japanese family in their home, there are several points of etiquette which you should observe.

- Take both your coat and shoes off in the hallway (*genkan*) before you enter the house itself. Arrange your shoes as you can see others are arranged.

- Try to take a small gift (a box of cakes or confectionery is traditional). This will be appreciated by your host.
- Don't offer to wash pots or dishes. As a guest you will not be expected to do so.
- After dinner, an appropriate comment to your host is *go-chiso-sama deshita* ('I have enjoyed my dinner very much' or 'Thank you for your hospitality.')

Colours

black	黒 *kuro*
red	赤 *aka*
navy blue	紺色 *kon'iro*
brown	茶色 *chairo*
white	白 *shiro*
yellow	黄色 *kiiro*
green	緑 *midori*

Shapes / katachi (形)

round	丸形／円形 *marugata/enkei*
square	真四角／正方形 *ma-shikaku/seihōkei*
oval	楕円形 *daen-kei*
diamond	菱形 *hishi-gata*
triangle	三角形 *sankaku-kei*

Countries

Australia	オーストラリア *ōsutoraria*
Austria	オーストリア *ōsutoria*
Belgium	ベルギー *berugī*
Canada	カナダ *kanada*
China	中国 *chūgoku*
Czechoslovakia	チェコスロバキア *chekosurobakia*
Denmark	デンマーク *denmāku*
England	イギリス *igirisu*
France	フランス *furansu*
Germany	ドイツ *doitsu*
Great Britain	英国 *eikoku*
Greece	ギリシャ *girisha*
Holland	オランダ *oranda*
Hungary	ハンガリー *hangarī*
India	インド *indo*
Ireland	アイルランド *airurando*
Italy	イタリア *itaria*

Essential Information

Japan	日本 *nihon/nippon*
Korea	韓国 *kankoku*
New Zealand	ニュージーランド *nyūjīrando*
Norway	ノルウェー *noruuē*
Pakistan	パキスタン *pakisutan*
Philippines	フィリピン *firipin*
Poland	ポーランド *pōrando*
Portugal	ポルトガル *porutogaru*
Roumania	ルーマニア *rūmania*
Spain	スペイン *supein*
Switzerland	スイス *suisu*
Turkey	トルコ *toruko*
USA	アメリカ（合衆国） *amerika (gasshūkoku)*
USSR	ソ連／ロシア *soren/roshia*
Yugoslavia	ユーゴスラビア *yūgosurabia*

To give your nationality add the suffix *jin* to the name of the country.

I am English	（私は）イギリス人です *(watashi wa) Igirisu-jin desu*

Important public signs

Pull	引く *hiku*
Push	押す *osu*
Entrance	入口 *iriguchi*
Exit	出口 *deguchi*
Emergency exit	非常口 *hijō-guchi*
Lavatory	便所／手洗い／トイレ／WC *benjo/tearai/toire/*WC
Men	男／殿方 *otoko/tonogata*
Women	女／婦人 *onna/fujin*
Restroom	化粧室 *keshō-shitsu*
No smoking	禁煙 *kin'en*
Caution	注意 *chūi*
Adult	大人 *otona*
Children	小人／子供 *shōjin/kodomo*
Underground railway	地下鉄 *chikatetsu*
Bank	銀行 *ginkō*
Money exchange	両替 *ryōgae*
Post box	ポスト *posuto*

Essential Information

Remove footwear	土足厳禁 *dosoku genkin*
Don't touch the exhibits	陳列品には手をふれるな *chinretsuhin niwa te o fureru na*
No parking	駐車禁止 *chūsha-kinshi*
No thoroughfare	行き止まり *iki-domari*
Road closed	通行止 *tsūkō-dome*
Unauthorized entry is forbidden	無断立入を禁ず *mudan-tachiiri o kinzu*
One way traffic	片側通行止 *katagawa tsūkō-dome*
Closed to all vehicles	諸車通行止 *Shosha tsūkō-dome*
Keep out	立入禁止 *tachiiri-kinshi*
Keep to the left	左側通行 *hidari gawa tsūkō*
Keep off the grass	芝生にて立入禁止 *shibafu nite tachiiri-kinshi*
Don't take photographs	写真撮影禁止 *shashin satsuei kinshi*
Please offer your seat to elderly or disabled people	お年寄りや体の不自由な方には席をゆずりましょう *o-toshiyori ya karada no fujiyū na kata niwa seki o yuzurimashō*
Traffic hold up	交通渋滞 *kōtsū jūtai*

WORDLIST

A

about ...goro/yaku/gurai
to accept tsukaeru/ukeireru
account kōza
ache itami
address jūsho
adult otona
aerogram earoguramu
after ...no ato ni/...go
ni
afternoon gogo
good afternoon konnichi
wa
age nenrei
air kūki
air conditioning eakon/
reibō
air mail kōkūbin
airport kūkō
airsickness hikōki yoi
air terminal kūkō no
tāminaru
alarm keihō
alcohol sake
allergy arerugi
alone/single hitori de
already mō/sude ni
always itsumo/tsune ni
ambulance kyūkyū – sha
America amerika/beikoku
American amerika –
jin/beikoku jin
ankle ashi-kubi
ant ari
antiseptic shōdoku – yaku
any ikutsuka no
anybody dare ka/dare mo
anything nani ka/nani mo
apartment apāto
appointment yoyaku

April shigatsu
area (place) basho
arm ude
to arrive tsuku/tōchaku
suru
ashtray haizara
to ask kiku/tazuneru
aspirin asupirin
asthma zensoku
at... ...de/...ni
at the end of ...no
shūten ni
attendant kakari-in/annai
– gakari
August hachigatsu
Australia ōsutoraria
automatic jidō no
automatically jidōteki ni
awful hidoi
it was awful hidokatta

B

at the back ushiro ni/kōhō
ni
bacon bēkon
bad warui
bag kaban
baggage nimotsu
to bake yaku
baker pan – ya
balance (bank) zandaka
balcony nikai sajiki
ball bōru
banana banana
bandage hōtai
bank ginkō
bank book yokin tsūchō
bar bā
barbecue bābekyū
baseball yakyū

basement   chikai
bathing resort   kaisui-
    yoku-jō
bathrobe   yukata
bathroom   yokushitsu/o-
    furo
batteries   denchi
to be   iru/aru
beach   kaigan
bean-jam bun   an – pan
beautiful   utsukushii/kirei
    na
bed   betto
  to go to bed   neru
bedclothes   shingu/yagu
bee   mitsubachi
beef   gyūniku/bīfu
  beef liver   gyū rebā
  beef roast   rōsuto bīfu
beer   bīru
before   mae ni
to begin   hajimaru
bicycle   jitensha
  bicycle racing   keirin
big   ōkii
bill   seikyūsho/kanjō
    (gaki)
birth   tanjo
birthday   tanjō-bi
biscuits   bisuketto
to bite   kamu/sasu
black   kuroi
blanket   mōfu
blouse   burausu
blue   aoi
book   hon
to book   yoyaku suru
book of tickets   kaisū ken
bookshop   hon – ya
boots   naga gutsu
boring   unzari suru/
    taikutsu na
to be born   umareru
bottle of   hitobin/ippon
box of matches   matchi hito
    hako

boy   otoko no ko
boyfriend   otoko
    tomodachi/bōi furendo
bra   burajā
brakes   burēki
brandy   burandē
to break   kowareru
breakfast   chōshoku
breast of chicken   tori no
    mune – niku
British   eikoku
    no/eikoku-jin
  a British person   eikoku –
    jin
brochure   panfuretto
broken   kowareta
brother (elder)   ani/onī
    san
  (younger)   otōto/otōto-
    san
buckwheat noodles   soba
bulb (electric)   denkyū
bullet train   shinkansen
to burn   yaku/moyasu/kogasu
burnt   kogeta
bus excursion   basu shūyū
    ryokō
bus station   basu teiryū –
    jo
business   shigoto
  business department
    eigyō – bu
but   shikashi/keredomo/
    . . . ga
butcher   niku – ya
butter   batā
to buy   kau
by . . .   . . . giwa/ . . . no
    soba ni/ . . . de

C
cake   kēki
calculator   keisan-ki/
    karikyurētā
to call   yobu/denwa o
    kakeru

145

call (telephone) denwa o
    kakeru koto/tsūwa
    (morning) mōningu
    kōru
camera kamera
Canada kanada
cap (hat) bōshi
car jidōsha/kuruma
    car park chūsha jō
card (business) meishi
caretaker kanri-nin
carp koi
to carry hakobu
cartoon (comic) manga
cash genkin
    cash desk kanjō-ba/reji
castle o-shiro
cat neko
to catch tsukamaeru
cavity (tooth) mushiba no
    ana
central heating danbō
centre chūshin
    town centre machi no
    chūshin
ceramics tōki/yakimono
to change (train & bus)
    norikaeru/(money)
    kaeru
change otsuri
charge daikin
to charge seikyū suru
cheap yasui
cheaper yori yasui
to check tenken
    suru/shiraberu
to check in chekku in suru
to check out kanjō o
    shiharatte deru
cheers kanpai
cheese chīzu
chemist's shop kusuri-ya
cheque (bank) kogitte
    (travellers) toraberāzu
    chekku
cheque card banku kādo

cherry sakuranbo
    cherry blossom sakura
chest mune
chicken (niwa) tori
    chicken meat tori
    niku/kei niku·
child kodomo
children kodomo-tachi
chocolate chokorēto
to choose kimeru/erabu
to chop kiru/kizamu
church kyōkai
cigarettes tabako
cinema eiga -kan
city shi/tokai
clam asari
to clean seisō suru
clean kirei na/seiketsu na
cleaner (vacuum) sōji-ki/
    kuri nā
clear meihaku na
cloakroom gaitō keitan-
    hin azukari-jo
to close shimeru
closet oshiire
clothes fuku
coat kōto
cod tara
coffee kōhī
    coffee shop kissa-ten
coin kōka/koin
    coin locker koin rokkā
cold (adj) tsumetai/samui
    (noun) kaze
collection shūshū
colour iro/karā
to come kuru
commission komisshon/
    tesūryō
company kaisha
to complain kujō ga
    aru/monku o iu
compound kongōbutsu/
    kongō zai
concert konsāto
to consist of kara naru

constipated benpi no
to contact renraku suru
contact lens kontakuto
  renzu
convenient benri na
to cook ryōri suru
cooking ryōri yō no
corner kōnā/sumi
counter kauntā
court (tennis) kōto
to cost hiyō ga kakaru
cost hiyō
cotton (noun) momen/men
  (adj) men no
cotton wool dasshimen
crab kani
cream kurīmu
  cream puff shū kurīmu
  cream bun kurīmu -pan
credit card kurejitto
  kādo
crockery setomono/tōki
croissant kurowassan
cucumber kyūri
cup kappu/koppu
currency tsūka
curry karē
custom zeikan
customers kyaku
cutlery hamono-rui
cutlet katsuretsu
cuttlefish ika

D
to dance dansu o
  suru/odoru
dark kurai
date hizuke
  date of birth seinen
  gappi
daughter musume(-san)
day hi
decayed tooth mushi ba
December jūnigatsu
to declare shinkoku suru
to delay okureru

delicious oishii
department (company) ...bu
  (store) depāto
departure shuppatsu
  departure lounge
  shuppatsu robī
deposit tetsuke kin/yokin
desk tsukue
details shōsai
detective tantei/keiji
to develop (film) genzō
  suru
diabetic tōnyōbyō (no)
diarrhoea geri
dining car shokudō – sha
dinner yūshoku
direct chokusetsu no/
  chokutsū no
discount waribiki
discounted waribiki sareta
dizzy memai ga suru
to do suru
documentary dokyumenta-
  rī
doll ningyō
dollar doru
  US amerika no doru
  Canadian kanada no
  doru
  Australian ōsutoraria no
  doru
double daburu na
doughnuts dōnatsu
dress doresu
dressing gown yukata
dried kansō shita
drink nomimono
to drive unten suru
driving licence unten
  menkyo shō
dry kawaita/mizu o
  tsukawanai
dry cleaning dorai
  kurīningu
duty free menzei no
duty free shop menzei-ten 147

Wordlist

E
early hayaku
earthquake jishin
to eat taberu
  to eat out gaishoku suru
eel unagi
egg tamago
electric denki no
electrician denki-ya
electricity denki
elevator erebētā
else hoka ni
emergency ōkyū no/kinkyū
  no
emergency exit hijō-guchi
end owari
to end owaru
engine enjin
England eikoku/igirisu
English (person) igirisu-jin
  (language) eigo
to enjoy tanoshimu
enough jūbun na.
entrance iriguchi
entry tachiiri
epileptic tenkan no
equipment yōgu/setsubi
escalator esukarētā
essential honshitsuteki na
evening yūkoku/higure/ban
  good evening konban wa
every . . .goto ni
everyday mainichi
everything zenbu/subete
to exchange ryōgae
  suru/kōkan suru
exchange ryōgae
  exchange bureau
    ryōgae-jo
  exchange rate kawase
    rēto
  exchange window
    kawase guchi
excursion shūyū
excuse me sumimasen/
  shitsurei desu ga

exhibition tenran-kai
exit deguchi
expensive nedan ga takai
to explain setsumei suru
express (train) kyūkō
express mail sokutatsu
expression hyōgen
extension (phone) naisen
extra yobun na
  extra charge warimashi
to extract (tooth) basshi
  suru
. . .exposure (film) . . .mai
  dori
eye me
  eye lotion megusuri
eyesight shiryoku

F
facilities shisetsu/setsubi
family kazoku
famous yūmei na
fan uchiwa/sensu
fantastic subarashii
far tōi
fare ryōkin
  fare adjustment office
    unchin seisan jo
fast hayai
father chichi/otō-san
fax machine fakushimiri
February nigatsu
to feel kanjiru
festival o-matsuri
fifth go-banme no
to fill mitasu
  to fill in kinyū suru
fillet hire/hire-niku
film (movie) eiga
  (photo) fuirumu
to find sagasu/mitsukeru
to finish owaru/shiageru
finish shiage
fire kaji/hi
first saisho no/ichiban me
  no

Wordlist

first class ittō no
fish sakana
fish-shop sakana-ya
flame waku
flight furaito
floor yuka/kai
flu infuruenza
folding fan sensu
to follow shitagau
football futto bōru/sakkā
for ...iki no/...no tame
  no
to forbid kinshi suru
foreign gaikoku no
fork hōku
form yōshi/yōshiki
forwarding ikusaki no
four yon/shi/yo/yottsu
fourth yon-ban me no
free aite iru
fresh shinsen na
fridge reizōko
fried itameta
  fried rice yaki-meshi
  fried noodles yaki-soba
friend tomodachi
frightening osoroshii
from... ...kara/
  ...shusshin no
fruit kudamono/furūtsu
  fruit juice furūtsu jūsu
  fruit shop kudamono-ya
full board ippaku nishoku-
  tsuki
funny omoshiroi
fuse hyūzu

G

game shiai/gēmu
gangster yakuza
garage garēji/shako
garden niwa
gas gasu
  gas worker gasu-ya
gate mon
  ticket gate kaisatsu-guchi

general ippan no
general manager buchō
to get eru
  to get to... ...ni tsuku
  to get on... ...ni noru
  to get off oriru
to gift wrap okurimono yō
  ni hōsō suru
gift okurimono/gifuto
gin jin
  gin and tonic jin tonikku
girl onna no ko/shōjo
girlfriend onna tomodachi/
  gāru furendo
to give ataeru/watasu
gizzard (chicken) sunazuri
glad ureshii
glass gurasu
  a glass of... ...ippai
glasses (spectacles) megane
glossy kōtaku no aru/tsuya
  no aru
to go iku
golf gorufu
good yoi
  good afternoon konnichi
    wa
  good-bye sayōnara
  good evening konban
    wa
  good morning ohayō
    -gozaimasu
  good night oyasumi
    nasai
gram guramu
grammar bunpō
grandchildren mago/o-
  mago-san
grandfather sofu/ojī-san
grandmother sobo/obā-san
grapes budō
great subarashii/idai na
green midori (no)
greengrocers yaoya
ground jimen/jō
  ground floor ikkai

149

guide annai
   guide book gaido bukku

H
hair kami no ke
haircut heyā katto
half hanbun no
half-board ippaku
   chōshoku-tsuki
half-time naka yasumi
hall hōru
ham hamu
hamburger hanbāgā
hand te
handbag hando bakku
to hate kirau
to have motsu/aru
he kare wa/kare ga
head atama
health kenkō
to hear kiku
heart shinzō
heavy omoi
   heavy rain ō-ame
to help tetsudau/tasukeru
help! tasuketē
herbal medicine kanpō
   yaku
here koko ni
him kare ni/kare o
to hire kariru
his kare no
hitch hiking hitchi haiku
hold the line shōshō
   o-machi kudasai
holiday horidei/kyūka
horrible hidoi
horse uma
   horse racing keiba
hospital byōin
hot atsui
   hot spring onsen
hotel hoteru
hour jikan
house ie/o-taku
how? donoyō ni/donna ni

how are you? o-genki desu
   ka/go-kigen ikaga desu
   ka
how long? dono kurai
how much? ikura
hungry onaka ga suita
hurt (adj) kega o
   shita/kizutsuita
to hurt itamu
husband (go) shujin

I
I watashi wa (ga)/boku wa
   (ga)/watakushi wa (ga)
   Yes, I am hai, sō desu
   No, I am not Iie, sō
   dewa arimasen
identification mibun
   shōmei
if moshi...naraba
ill byōki de/kibun ga
   warui
immediately sugu
   ni/tadachi ni
immigration shutsu
   nyūkoku kanri
important jūyō na/taisetsu
   na
in ...no naka ni.../
   ...ni.../...de.../
   ...dewa...
to include hukumu/hairu
indoor shitsunai no
inexpensive takakunai/yas
   ui
information annai/jōhō
injection chūsha
insect konchū/mushi
inside ...no naka niwa
interest kyōmi/rishi
interesting omoshiroi/
   kyōmi bukai
interval makuai/kyūkei
   jikan
into ...no naka e
is desu

it sore wa (ga)/sore
   o/sore ni
item kōmoku

J
jam jamu
to jam ugokanaku
   naru/koshō suru
January ichigatsu
Japan nihon/nippon
Japanese (language) nihon-
   go
  (people) nihon-jin
Japan Rail JR/kokutetsu
jeans jīpan
judo jūdō
jug jokki
juice jūsu
July shichigatsu
to jump tobu
June rokugatsu
just (right) chōdo (ii)

K
key kagi
  key-money kenri-kin
kilometre kiromētoru
kiosk baiten
knife naifu
to know shiru/wakaru

L
lacquerware shikki
lake mizuumi
landlord yanushi
lane sen/shasen
lantern chōchin
last night kinō no yoru/
   sakuya
last year kyonen/sakunen
late osoi
laundrette koin randorī
leaflet rīfuretto
leather kawa

to leave shuppatsu suru/
   nokosu/deru/hassha
   suru
left hidari
left luggage office
   tenimotsu ichiji azukari
   jo
leg ashi
lens renzu
less yori sukunai
lesson jugyō
let's... sā...shimashō
letter tegami
license menkyo
lift erebētā
light (colour) usui
  (weight) karui
light bulb denkyū
lighter raitā
like (as)... ...no yō na
to like konomu/suku
  I like it suki desu
limit genkai
list ichiran-hyō
little sukoshi
litre rittoru
to live sumu/ikiru
liver rebā/kanzō
lobster ise ebi
local train futsū ressha
locker rokkā
long nagai
long-sighted enshi no
to look miru
  to look for sagasu
to lose nakusu/ushinau
lost property ishitsu butsu
lounge robī
luggage nimotsu
lunch chūshoku

Wordlist

M

machine kikai
mackerel saba
to be made of... ...de tsukurarete iru/...sei de aru
maid (hotel) jochū
mail yūbin
  airmail kōkūbin
  surface mail funabin
to make tsukuru/...ni naru
  to make contact renraku suru
manager (hotel) shihainin
  general manager buchō
map chizu
March sangatsu
market ichiba
matinee performance hiru kōgyō
May gogatsu
may I...? ...shitemo ii desu ka
meal shokuji
  after meal shoku go
  before meal shoku zen
me watashi ni (o)
meat niku
mechanism (kikai) sōchi
medicine kusuri
medium chūkurai
to meet au
meeting kaigi
melon meron
men hitobito/otoko no hito
to mention shuchō suru
  don't mention it dō itashimashite
message dengon/kotozute
metal kinzoku
metre mētoru
middle mannaka
  middle-sized car chūgata-sha

milk gyūnyū/miruku
to mind kamau/ki o tsukeru
minced beef gyū minchi
minced chicken tori minchi
minute fun/pun
mistake machigai
to mix mazeru
mixed mikkusu sareta
mixture moriawase
moment (at the) genzai
Monday getsuyōbi
monetary value kingaku
monthly maitsuki
money o-kane
month tsuki
  one month ikkagetsu
more yori ōi
morning asa
  in the morning gozen chū (ni)
  this morning kesa
mother haha/okā-san
motorway kōsoku dōro
mouth kuchi
mountain yama
Mr/Mrs/Miss san
much (adj) ōku no/takusan no
much (adv) ōi ni/taisō
  how much? ikura
museum hakubutsu kan
musical myūjikaru
must I...? ...shinakereba narimasenka
mustard karashi
my watashi no

N

name namae/shimei
narrow semai
nationality kokuseki
navy blue kon iro
near (no) chikaku ni/...hen ni
nearest moyori no

to need   iru/hitsuyō de aru
needle   hari
new   atarashii
news   shirase/nyūsu
newspaper   shinbun
next   tsugi no/jikai no
night   yoru/ban
  good night   oyasumi
        nasai
  one night   ippaku
nine   kyū/ku
nineteen   jū-kyū/jū-ku
no   iie
  no parking   chūsha kinshi
  no smoking   kin'en
noodles   soba/udon
not allowed   kinshi sarete
        iru/kyoka sarete inai
notepaper   nōto
notes (money)   shihei/satsu
nothing   nanimonai
to notice   ki ga tsuku
noun   meishi
November   jūichigatsu
now   ima/genzai
number   bangō/ban
nylon   nairon

O
o'clock   . . . ji
October   jūgatsu
octopus   tako
office   jimusho
often   shibashiba/tabitabi
  how often   do no kurai no
        hindo de nanpun oki ni
oil   oiru
old   furui/toshitotta
  how old . . . ?   nan-sai
omelette   omuretsu
on . . .   . . . no ue ni/ . . . ni
one   hitotsu/ippō no
onions   tamanegi
only   . . . shika/ . . . dake/
        tada/tan ni
open   aite iru/aita

opinion   iken
optician   megane-ya
to order   chūmon
        suru/tanomu
original   orijinaru no
other   hoka no/ta no
our   watashi-tachi no
out   gaishutsu chū no . . .
outdoor   okugai no
over   . . . o koete/mukō no
        hō ni
  over there   asoko
overcoat   ōbā
overcooked   yakesugi
        nisugi

P
a packet of . . .   . . . hito-
        hukuro/ . . . hito-hako
pain   itami
pamphlets   panfuretto
pan   nabe
pancake (Japanese style)
        okonomiyaki
a pair of . . .   ittsui
  .   hitokumi
panties   panti
pants   pantsu
paper   pēpā/kami
parcel   kozutsumi
parent   oya/oyago-san
parents   ryōshin/go-ryōshin
party   pāti/ikkō
passenger   jōkyaku
  passenger ticket   jōsha-ken
passport   pasupōto/ryoken
path   michi
to pay   harau/shiharau
payment   shiharai
peach   momo
pear   nashi
pearl   shinju
penicillin   penishirin
people   hitobito
performance   kōgyō/jōen/
        jikkō

153

Wordlist

perfume kōsui
persimmon kaki
period kikan/jidai
person hito
personal shiyō no
personnel jin'in/jin ji bu
   personnel manager jinji kachō
petrol gasorin
   petrol station gasorin sutando
phone denwa
to phone denwa o kakeru
phone card telefon kādo
photo shashin
photography shashin jutsu
piano piano
to pick hirou
picture e
piece hitokire/ippen
pill hinin'yaku
pillow makura
PIN number anshō bangō
place basho/tokoro
plastic purasuchikku
plate o-sara
platform hōmu
please dōzo
   yes, please Hai, o-negai shimasu
plumber suidō-ya
pocket poketto
police omawari/keikan
   police box kōban
pork buta niku
   pork fillet buta hire niku
portable keitai yō no
post yūbinbutsu
   post card hagaki
   post office yūbin-kyoku
potato jagaimo
pottery tōki/yakimono
pound (£) pondo
prawn ebi
to prefer ...no hō ga ii...
prescription shohōsen

present (gift) purezento/okurimono
pressure atsuryoku
   (blood) ketsuatsu
price kakaku/nedan
private kojin no
problem mondai
programme puroguramu
pronunciation hatsuon
property shoyū-butsu
pure junsui no
to put in... ireru
to put on... ni noseru ...o tsukeru
pyjamas pajama

Q
question shitsumon
quiet shizuka na
quite kanari/hijō ni

R
racing (horse) keiba
   (bike) keirin
radish daikon
railway tetsudō
   railway station tetsudō eki
   railway ticket jōsha-ken
to rain ame ga furu
rainy season tsuyu
rapid (express) kyūsoku no/hayai
rare steak nama yake no sutēki (reā no)
rate rēto/sōba
   exchange rate kawase rēto/kawase sōba
raw nama no
ready dekiagatta/junbi no dekita
receipt ryōshū-sho
to recommend suisen suru
rectangular nagashikaku/chōhōkei

red   aka
reduced rate   waribiki
reduction   sashihiki
refund   harai-modoshi
to register   tōroku suru
registered mail   kakidome
registration   tōroku
to release   fūgiri suru/kōkai
   suru
to rent   kariru
rental   chintai no
rental car   renta kā
to repack   konpō shinaosu
to repair   shūri suru
to repeat   kurikaesu
reservation   yoyaku
to reserve   yoyaku suru
reserved seat   shitei seki
resort   kōraku-chi/rizōto
   (bathing)   kaisui-
      yoku-jo
restaurant   resutoran
to return   kaeru/modosu
return ticket   ōfuku kippu
rice   kome/gohan
right (correct)   tadashii
   (direction)   migi
ring   yubiwa
   (telephone)   denwa suru
road   dōro/michi
roasted   rōsuto sareta
roe (fish)   sakana no
   tamago
   (salmon)   ikura
roll   maki/maite aru
   mono
romance   ren'ai/bōken
   monogatari
room   heya
rosé (wine)   rōze wain
round   marugata/enkei
   round trip   ōfuku ryokō
      (no)
row   retsu
rubbish   gomi
to run   hashiru

S
safe (adj)   anzen na
   (noun)   kinko
sake   sake
salmon   sake
salt   shio
salty   shio karai
same   onaji
sandwich   sandoitchi/sando
sanitary   eisei jō no
sardine   iwashi
satsuma   mikan
Saturday   doyōbi
sauce   sōsu
sausage   sōsēji
to say   iu/kataru
screen   sukurīn
screw-driver   daraibā/neji
   -mawashi
sea-bream   tai
sea-eel   anago
season   kisetsu
seat   seki
sea-urchin   uni
second   ni-banme no
section   ka/bumon
to see   au/miru
   I'm glad to see you   dōzo
      yoroshiku/o-me ni
      kakarete ureshii desu
to sell   uru
to send   okuru
September   kugatsu
to serve   kyūshi o
   suru/dasu
service   sābisu-ryō
shall we...?   ...shimashō
   ka/sābisu
shape   katachi
shell fish   kai-rui
shirts   waishatsu
shivery   samui/furueru
shoes   kutsu/shūzu
shop   mise
shopping   shoppingu/
   kaim-ono

shopping centre shōten-
  gai/shoppingu sentā
shop-soiled tanazarashi no
short mijikai
short-sighted kinshi no
should subeki da
to show miseru/shimesu
shower shawā
shrimp ebi
sick byōki no
  to feel sick hakike ga
    suru/kibun ga warui
to sign sain suru
signature shomei
silk kinu
single hitori yō no/tatta
    hitotsu no
  (unmarried) dokushin
    no/mikon no
  (ticket) katamichi no
silver gin
sister (elder) ane/onē-san
  (younger) imōto/imōto-
    san
to sit suwaru
six roku/mittsu/rokko
size sunpō/saizu
sized saizu no
skate sukēto
skirt sukāto
to ski sukī o suru
skiing sukī o suru koto
sledge sori
to sleep neru
sleeping car shindai-sha
to slice usugiri suru
slide suraido
slope(s) surōpu/keisha-
    men/saka
slowly yukkuri
small chiisai/shōryō no
  small sized kogata no
to smoke tabako o suu
smoking kitsuen
  non-smoking kin'en
156 **snacks** keishoku

soap sekken
socks kutsushita
soft sofuto na/yawarakai
sole kutsu zoko
some ikutsuka no/ikura ka
    no
somebody dare ka/donata
    ka
someone dare ka/donata
    ka
something nani ka
son musuko/musuko-san
soon mamonaku/sugu
sore itai
sorry (hard luck) kinodoku
    na/zannen na
  I'm sorry sumimasen/
    gomen nasai
sound oto
soy bean daizu
  soy bean curd tōfu/dōfu
soy sauce shōyu
spare supeā no
to speak hanasu
special tokubetsu no
spectacles megane
speed spīdo/hayasa
to spend tsuiyasu/tsukau
sport undō/supōtsu
square mashikaku/seihōkei
squid ika
stage butai/dankai
staircase kaidan
stall ikkai zenpō
stamp kitte/inkan
stand (taxi) noriba
standard hyōjun no
statement meisaisho
station (railway) eki
stationer's bunbōgu-ya
station kiosk eki no baiten
to stay taizai suru
steak sutēki
stew shichū
to step out seki o hazusu
sticking tape bansōkō

stick bō/tsue/sutekki
  (ski) sutokku
to sting sasu
stomach i/hukubu
stop tomeru koto teiryū-jo
to stop tomaru/yameru
store (shop) mise
stove sutōbu
straight (on) massugu
straight away tadachi
  ni/sugu ni
strawberry ichigo/
  sutoroberi
street dōro/michi
strong tsuyoi
tudent gakusei
o study benkyō suru
ub-titles midashi
uit fuku/sebiro
uitcase sūtsukēsu
umo wrestling sumō no
  torikumi
unday nichiyōbi
unglasses san-gurasu
unstroke nissha-byō
upermarket sūpā-māketto
urface mail funabin
urgery shinsatsu/shinryō
  shitsu
weater sētā
weet amai/amakuchi no
welling hare (mono)
wimming pool pūru
wimming trunks kaisui
  pantsu
vimsuit suieigi/mizugi
vord katana

ble tēburu
blet jōzai
• take uketoru
  (a taxi etc) noru
  (time) kakaru
  (objects) motte iku
  (photos) shashin o toru

to take off ririku
  suru/shuppatsu suru
tampon tanpon
tank tanku
tasty oishii
tax zeikin
taxi takushī
tea o-cha
  tea ceremony cha no yu
teacher sensei
telegram denpō
telephone denwa
temperature ondo/taion
temple o-tera/bukkaku
tender yawarakai
tennis tenisu
terminal tāminaru
to test kensa suru/shiken o
  suru
than... ...yori
  more than... ...yori
  ōku/...ijō
thank you arigatō
  (gozaimasu)
  no, thank you iie, kekkō
  desu
that sore/sono
that (over there) are/ano
theatre gekijō/shibai goya
their kare-ra/kanojo-
  ra/sore-ra no
them kare-ra/kanojo-
  ra/sore-ra o (ni)
there soko
  over there asoko
there is/are ...ga imasu/
  ...ga arimasu
these kore-ra/kore-ra
  no/kore/kono
they kare-ra/kanojo-
  ra/sore-ra wa (ga)
thick atsui/futoi
thickly atsuku
thin usui
thing mono/koto
to think omou/kangaeru

157

thinly usuku
third san-banme no
thirsty nodo ga kawaita
this kore/kono
  this morning kesa
those sore-ra/sore-ra
    no/sore/sono
those over there are-ra/are-
    ra no/are/ano
thousand sen
thread ito
three san/mittsu
throat nodo
Thursday mokuyōbi
ticket kippu
  tickets (a book of)
      kaisū-ken
  ticket-gate kaisatsu-guchi
  ticket office kippu-uriba
tights taitsu
till... ...made
time jikan/...kai
  what time? nan-ji
to toast tōsuto suru/yaku
tobacconist tabako-ya
today kyō
together ...to issho ni
toilet benjo/toire/tearai
tomato tomato
tomorrow asu/ashita
tonic tonikku
tonight kon'ya
too (adj) ...sugiru
  (also) ...mo
tooth ha
toothache shitsū
total gōkei/zenbu
    no/zentai no
tough (meat) katai
  (character) shin ga tsuyoi
tour ryokō/shūyū
tourist ryokōsha/kankō-
    kyaku
towel taoru/te-nugui
town machi/shi
158 toy omocha

traditional dentōteki na
traffic kōtsū/tsūkō
  one-way traffic ippō
      tsūkō
train ressha/kissha
  (bullet) shinkansen
transfer kuriire
to travel ryokō suru
travel bureau ryokō annai
    jo/kōtsū kōsha
traveller ryokōsha
traveller's cheque
    toraberāzu chekku
treat sochi
trousers zubon
trout masu
true hontō no/tadashii
T-shirt tī-shatsu
Tuesday kayōbi
tuna maguro
to turn magaru
TV terebi
to twist nenza suru/nejiru
    mageru
two ni/futatsu
typhoon taifū
tyre taiya

U
umbrella kasa
underground chikatetsu
underpants pantsu
to understand wakaru/
    rikai suru
unleaded muen no
USA amerika
US dollars amerika no
    doru
useful yaku ni tatsu/yūek
    na
usually futsū

Wordlist

V

vacant (taxi) kūsha
vacuum shinkū (no)
  vacuum cleaner denki
    sōjiki
vehicles kuruma/sharyō/
    yusō-kikan
veranda beranda
very hidoku/hijō ni/
    totemo
vinegar su
to visit otozureru/hōmon
    suru
visitor hōmon-sha/kanko-
    kyaku

W

to wait matsu
waiting room machiai-
    shitsu
walks sanpo-michi
wallet saifu/satsu-ire
to want iru/hossuru/
    nozumu
to want to... shitai/
    ...shitagaru
was deshita
to wash arau
wash basin senmen-ki
washing sentaku-mono
washing machine sentaku-
    ki
watch tokei
water mizu
way (road) michi
we watashi-tachi wa (ga)
to wear (clothes) kiru
Wednesday suiyōbi
week (for a) is-shukan
weekly isshūkan ni/
    tsuki/maishū
well yoku/umaku
  well done yoku yaketa/
    uerudan no
western (film) seibu-geki
whale kujira

what nani/donna mono
    (koto)
  what floor nan-kai
  what sort of donna
when itsu
where doko
which dono/dochira
whisky uisukī
  and water mizuwari
while shibaraku
who dare
  (polite) donata
  (telephone) dochira-
    sama/donata
whole zentai no/marugoto
why naze/dōshite
wide haba no hiroi
wife tsuma/kanae/oku-san
will you?... ...shite
    kudasaimasu ka/shite
    moraemasu ka
to wind maku
  wind-bells fūrin
window mado/madoguchi
wine wain/budō-shu
  wine store sakaya
to wrap tsutsumu
wrestlers (sumo) sekitori
wrestling (sumo) torikumi
to write kaku
  to write down kinyū
    suru
writing paper hikki yōshi
with to/to issho ni/ga
    aru/tsuki no
withdrawal harai modoshi
    kin
without ...ga nai
woman josei/onna no hito
wonderful subarashii
wooden ki no/mokusei no
wool yōmō
  cotton wool dasshimen
word kotoba/tango
to work ugoku/hataraku
  to work for ni tsutomeru 159

worker sagyō-in / jūgyō-in
I would like o o-negai
    shimasu / o kudasai

Y
yacht yotto
year nen / toshi
  last year kyonen /
    sakunen

  next year rainen
yellow kiiro
yen en
yesterday kinō / sakujitsu
you anata / anata-
    tachi / anata-gata (wa,
    ga, o, ni)
your anata / anata-
    tachi / anata-gata no